REEL ADVENTURES

REEL ADVENTURES

The Savvy Teens' Guide to Great Movies

John Lekich

ANNICK PRESS

TORONTO + NEW YORK + VANCOUVER

Copyright © 2002 John Lekich

Annick Press Ltd.

All rights reserved. No part of this work covered by the copyrights hereon may be reproduced or used in any form or by any means – graphic, electronic, or mechanical – without the prior written permission of the publisher.

We acknowledge the support of the Canada Council for the Arts, the Ontario Arts Council, and the Government of Canada through the Book Publishing Industry Development Program (BPIDP) for our publishing activities.

Edited by Barbara Pulling
Copy-edited by Lesley Cameron
Cover and interior design by Irvin Cheung/iCheung Design
Dean cover photograph CP/AP; Witherspoon and Washington cover photographs
Mégapress Images.

Cataloguing in Publication Data

Lekich, John
    Reel adventures: the savvy teens' guide to great movies

ISBN 1-55037-735-3

    1. Motion pictures—Catalogs. I. Title.

PN1998.L43 2002   016.79143'75   C2002-901125-6

The text was typeset in Perpetua, Eurostile & Meta

Distributed in Canada by	**Published in the U.S.A. by**	**Distributed in the U.S.A. by**
Firefly Books Ltd.	Annick Press (U.S.) Ltd.	Firefly Books (U.S.) Inc.
3680 Victoria Park Avenue		P.O. Box 1338
Willowdale, ON		Ellicott Station
M2H 3K1		Buffalo, NY 14205

Printed and bound in Canada

visit us at **www.annickpress.com**

Table of Contents

For Janet, my first companion at the movies.

Introduction

⭐ ⭐ ⭐ ⭐ ⭐

I've been watching movies since I was old enough to sit still and I enjoyed the experience so much that I ended up reviewing movies for a living. You might think that watching so many movies would make choosing the films to include in this book a lot easier, but it was tough narrowing down the list. Frankly, you have to be a little crazy even to try. There's no way you can put together a guide like this and not leave out a lot of good stuff. But, if there's one thing I was striving for, it's variety. I like every film included here for any number of reasons but they all have one thing in common — good movies cut across time, space, and a multitude of hairstyles to make sure that your time in front of the screen takes you to a place you've always wanted to go. You just don't know it yet.

The movies in *Reel Adventures* range from the latest blockbusters to vintage classics that have stood the test of time. If awards mean anything to you, there are enough Oscar-winners included in this volume to fill a couple of Winnebagos. There are also many lesser-known gems. All the films take risks and all of them have something to say that's worth hearing over the crunch of popcorn.

Most memorable films tend to have certain elements that stand out—inspiring acting, an exotic setting, or awesome special effects. But they also have a way of defying categories. They can shock you, thrill you, make you laugh, or change how you think about life in a fundamental way. Sometimes they can accomplish all these things at once. All any of them ask is that you leave yourself open to the worlds they create. In return, you'll be rewarded with a universe of possibilities. Enjoy.

How to Use This Book

★ ★ ★ ★ ★

The films in this book are divided into five categories: "Getting There," "The Great Escape," "Think about It," "Fright Night," and "Just for Laughs." At the end of each section is a list of ten classics, groundbreaking movies or cult favorites that I have a particular affection for. Some may already be favorites of yours. But, if you haven't seen them, you can look forward to discovering some of the best movies ever made in the long and rich history of film.

The individual entry for each film contains the following information:

Title (year)
Director, Names of principal actors.

THE SHORT STORY ★ A combined plot synopsis and opinion that cuts to the chase.

MEMORABLE MOMENT OR LINE ★ A line or moment in the film that you should watch for.

MESSAGE ★ What the film is trying to say. Or, in some cases, what the film is saying inadvertently.

For some films, I've also included a category called **CHECK THIS OUT** ★ which suggests a worthwhile movie with a similar theme or, in some cases, the same actor or director. The sidebars scattered throughout the book highlight interesting tidbits about particular films or actors.

For quick reference, the index at the end of the book gives you access to movies by titles and principal actors.

Getting There

★ ★ ★ ★ ★

There's a genre that some critics like to call the coming-of-age film, movies that deal with the struggle to cope in a changing world while you're still trying to figure out your life. But the subjects covered by the films in this category are much broader than that — you'll find everything from a guy who builds rockets to a young woman who finds her life empowered through dance. Everybody needs a dream. What these movies are about is the attempt to make those dreams come true.

Baby, It's You (1983)

Directed by John Sayles.

Starring Rosanna Arquette, Vincent Spano, Joanna Merlin.

THE SHORT STORY ★ A romantic relationship tries to survive past graduation. Limited but charming guy falls for smart, ambitious girl. They say that opposites attract, but John Sayles knows such attraction can buckle under social pressure. This is a bittersweet examination of how different goals can pull us apart as we grow older. If you've ever been inexplicably drawn to someone who's totally wrong for you, you'll relate to this movie.

MEMORABLE MOMENT ★ Our hero lip-syncing to Frank Sinatra.

MESSAGE ★ Don't expect love to conquer all.

Big (1988)

Directed by Penny Marshall.

Starring Tom Hanks, Elizabeth Perkins, John Heard.

THE SHORT STORY ★ A frustrated 12-year-old named Josh wishes he was big and then wakes up the next morning as a man in his 30s. The problem? He still thinks like a 12-year-old, even though he has the body of a mature male. Cut off from his parents and friends, he's forced to find his way in the sophisticated world of adults. Other movies have tried the same concept with limited success. This one works because it treats the subject of growing up with care and respect.

MEMORABLE MOMENT ★ Big Josh (Tom Hanks) helping to play a duet on a giant piano by dancing on the keys.

MESSAGE ★ What's your hurry?

Billy Elliot (2000)

Directed by Stephen Daldry.

Starring Jamie Bell, Julie Walters, Jamie Draven.

THE SHORT STORY ★ Young Billy Elliot lives in an English mining town where the rules of social behavior are simple. Rule number one? Guys do boxing. But after Billy stumbles upon a dance class, he discovers an unexpected talent for ballet. Although his no-nonsense instructor encourages this new interest, Billy's dad is horrified that his youngest son wants to prance around in toeshoes. A striking miner, he refuses to waste precious money on something as objectionable as ballet lessons. But his son is tougher than he realizes.

MEMORABLE MOMENT ★ An angry Billy blowing off steam by dancing through the streets.

MESSAGE ★ Sometimes you find your dream, and sometimes it finds you.

Growing up

Kirsten Dunst (*Deeply, Bring It On*) made her debut in a TV commercial at the age of three. But her big break came in 1994's *Interview with a Vampire: The Vampire Chronicles*. As a blood-sucking creature of the night, she delivered her first screen kiss to actor Brad Pitt. Dunst has said: "Boys frustrate me. I hate all their indirect messages. I hate game playing. Do you like me or don't you? Just tell me so I can get over you."

Bottle Rocket (1996)

Directed by Wes Anderson.

Starring Owen C. Wilson, Luke Wilson, James Caan.

THE SHORT STORY ★ This one will make you think twice before embarking on a thrilling life in petty crime. Two friends set out to learn about larceny with less than impressive results. James Caan co-stars as a charismatic crook who teaches the boys a lesson. Fresh and original with a touch of nostalgia.

MEMORABLE MOMENT ★ How Caan takes advantage of his young proteges.

MESSAGE ★ A life of crime isn't for everybody.

CHECK THIS OUT ★ For another interesting film from director Wes Anderson, try the 1998 comedy *Rushmore*.

The Breakfast Club (1985)

Written and directed by John Hughes.

Starring Emilio Estevez, Judd Nelson, Molly Ringwald.

THE SHORT STORY ★ Five high-school students get to know each other while serving Saturday detention together. Writer-director John Hughes goes deeper than you might expect here. Yes, there are laughs, but this is also a sincere attempt to go beyond superficial stereotypes and venture into more complex emotional territory. Maybe that's why *The Breakfast Club* wears better than some teen-oriented films made around the same time. Don't miss this one.

MEMORABLE LINE ★ "Will milk be made available to us?"

MESSAGE ★ Get to know someone before passing judgment.

Breaking Away (1979)

Directed by Peter Yates.

Starring Dennis Christopher, Paul Dooley, Daniel Stern.

THE SHORT STORY ★ Small-town guy Dave (Christopher) is obsessed with becoming a champion bicycle racer. Dooley is hilarious as his dad, a grumpy used-car salesman who's convinced his working-class son is aiming way too high for his own good. Dave's slacker friends aren't exactly an inspiration either; at least until they decide to challenge the local college snobs in the yearly bike race. I've actually seen people stand up and cheer during the finale. Catch this one and discover why.

MEMORABLE MOMENT ★ Dave's dad catches him shaving his legs.

MESSAGE ★ Take pride in who you are.

Chariots of Fire (1981)

Directed by Hugh Hudson.

Starring Ben Cross, Ian Charleson, Nigel Havers.

THE SHORT STORY ★ An entertaining psychological study, based on a true story, of two runners who compete in the 1924 Olympics. One is a Scottish missionary and the other a student at Cambridge, the famous British university. Part sports movie and part history lesson, this is a spirited tribute to a simpler time. The theme by Vangelis has become musical shorthand for the idea of triumphing over adversity.

MEMORABLE LINE ★ "God made me for a purpose. When I run I feel His pleasure. To win is to honor Him."

MESSAGE ★ It takes more than pure athletic ability to be the best.

CHECK THIS OUT ★ For another movie about running, try 1998's *Without Limits*.

The Commitments (1991)

Directed by Alan Parker.

Starring Robert Arkins, Michael Aherne, Angeline Ball.

Based on the novel by Roddy Doyle.

THE SHORT STORY ★ Young, working-class Dubliners decide to form a group that performs classic soul music. Things get complicated when ego problems and personal difficulties create tension within the band. The story's a treat. And can these people sing or what! The movie's infectious charm is matched only by the killer soundtrack.

MEMORABLE LINE ★ "What are your influences?"

MESSAGE ★ You gotta have soul.

CHECK THIS OUT ★ The film version of Roddy Doyle's *The Snapper* (1993)

Dazed and Confused (1993)

Directed by Richard Linklater.

Starring Jason London, Wiley Wiggins, Sasha Jensen.

THE SHORT STORY ★ A slice of '70s life via a diverse group of Texas high-school students. Director Linklater doesn't soften the pain of adolescence or the way some people choose to cope with it. Among the accomplished cast you'll spot Ben Affleck in an early role.

MEMORABLE LINE ★ "Check ya later!"

MESSAGE ★ If you want to preserve your high-school memories, make sure you buy a yearbook.

CHECK THIS OUT ★ Spike Lee's 1988 take on campus life, *School Daze*.

Diner (1982)

Written and directed by Barry Levinson.

Starring Steve Guttenberg, Daniel Stern, Mickey Rourke.

THE SHORT STORY ★ A bunch of friends struggle to find their place in the world while hanging out at a local diner. This funny and often poignant movie takes place in '50s Baltimore. Writer-director Levinson gets the period details just right. Much of the young cast went on to thriving careers in the '80s and beyond.

MEMORABLE MOMENT ★ The football test.

MESSAGE ★ Your friends can help you through life's rough spots.

Dirty Dancing (1987)

Directed by Emile Ardolino.

Starring Jennifer Grey, Patrick Swayze, Jerry Orbach.

THE SHORT STORY ★ A surprise hit on its initial release, this coming-of age tale keeps finding new generations of fans on video. At a Catskills resort in the '60s, a sheltered teenager learns about life and love when she encounters a troupe of free-spirited entertainers. Lively dance numbers and a romantic point of view blend nicely with an underlying social message about crossing over to the wrong side of the tracks. Jennifer Grey stars as the doctor's daughter who learns to loosen up by hitting the dance floor.

MEMORABLE MOMENT ★ Any dance number.

MESSAGE ★ You'll never get anywhere unless you take a chance.

Double Happiness (1994)

Written and directed by Mina Shum.

Starring Sandra Oh, Stephen Chang, Callum Keith Rennie.

THE SHORT STORY ★ Jade (Oh) is a young Chinese-Canadian woman trying to gain independence from her strict parents while maintaining a loving relationship with them. A sweet, heartfelt look at the clash between contemporary values and family tradition. The great thing about this film is that it shows us both sides of the story.

MEMORABLE MOMENT ★ Jade sweeping the floor while singing "Kung-Fu Fighting."

MESSAGE ★ Breaking away is hard to do.

The Flamingo Kid (1984)

Directed by Garry Marshall.

Starring Matt Dillon, Richard Crenna, Hector Elizondo.

THE SHORT STORY ★ Matt Dillon stars as Jeffrey Willis, an impressionable young man who learns a valuable lesson while working at a beach resort. When Jeffrey falls for the flashy line of a self-important car dealer, it looks like his life is going to veer off track. This entertaining morality tale features a memorable performance by Richard Crenna as the kind of guy who thinks a fat wallet is the ultimate goal in life. Great period feel for the early '60s.

MEMORABLE LINE ★ Crenna's character advises Jeffrey to forget about educational enlightenment. "You've never seen a philosopher making fifty grand a year …"

MESSAGE ★ Money isn't the most important thing in life.

Flashdance (1983)

Directed by Adrian Lyne.

Starring Jennifer Beals, Michael Nouri, Lilia Skala.

THE SHORT STORY ★ The only box-office blockbuster ever made about a female welder who aspires to be a dancer. Jennifer Beals stars as the nimble Alex Owens. Wielding a blowtorch by day, she longs to find a home for her unique brand of choreography. Her hunky boss (Nouri) decides to lend a helping hand after seeing her perform. Director Lyne loads the film with impressive visuals. Think of this as an extended rock video with the heart of an old-fashioned musical. Parodied often, but still packs a punch.

MEMORABLE LINE ★ Alex on losing herself in dance: "I just can't wait to get out there so I can disappear."

MESSAGE ★ Like the song says: "What a feeling!"

The Freshman (1990)

Directed by Andrew Bergman.

Starring Matthew Broderick, Marlon Brando, Maximilian Schell.

THE SHORT STORY ★ Matthew Broderick stars as a film student who gets tangled up in the life of a Mafia boss. (Who else but Marlon Brando?) An appealing, low-key comedy that works because of the obvious chemistry between the two leads. This is Brando's most sincere performance since his comeback role in *The Godfather*. That alone has to be worth the price of a video rental.

MEMORABLE MOMENT ★ The explanation of what really happened to the painting of the Mona Lisa.

MESSAGE ★ A part-time job can take you to places you never expected.

Ghost World (2001)

Directed by Terry Zwigoff.

Starring Thora Birch, Scarlett Johansson, Steve Buscemi.

THE SHORT STORY ★ A bittersweet tale of two precocious teens who get involved in the life of a lonely middle-aged man. What they're really doing is trying to spice up their own lives. This one has much to say about how friends can drift apart when they develop different interests. Funny and important, this is a film with a message that should last.

MEMORABLE MOMENT ★ Spying in the coffee shop.

MESSAGE ★ You can't hang on to high school forever, even though you may want to.

Treading the boards

In addition to starring in films, New Yorker **Matthew Broderick** has also made a name for himself on the Broadway stage. He has starred in the musicals *How to Succeed in Business Without Really Trying* and *The Producers*.

girlfight (2000)

Directed by Karyn Kusama.

Starring Michelle Rodriguez, Jaime Tirelli, Paul Calderon.

THE SHORT STORY ★ *Rocky* with a twist. The fighter in the ring is a girl. Actually, there's a lot more going on here than boxing. This is the story of a young Hispanic woman who uses the sport to blow off emotional steam. In the process, she learns a lot about discipline, self-respect, and other good things.

MEMORABLE MOMENT ★ Training in the ring.

MESSAGE ★ Be a contender in life.

CHECK THIS OUT ★ For another spin on boxing, try 2000's *Price of Glory.*

The Great Santini (1979)

Directed by Lewis John Carlino.

Starring Robert Duvall, Michael O'Keefe, Blythe Danner.

Based on the book by Pat Conroy.

THE SHORT STORY ★ This movie examines the complex relationship between a domineering father and his sensitive son. Robert Duvall is superb as a bullying military man who takes out his frustrations on his family. For all the tension, you can still see how much father and son want to love each other.

MEMORABLE MOMENT ★ Shooting hoops.

MESSAGE ★ Love hurts.

Teenage kicks

Johnny Depp told a magazine writer that during his teenage years, "I literally locked myself in a room and played guitar." Depp has performed in a couple of bands over the years and plays a mean guitar in the film *Chocolat.* Actress **Winona Ryder** inspired a love-struck **Depp** to get a tattoo that read "Winona Forever." After they broke up, he had the tattoo altered to read: "Wino Forever."

Hoosiers (1986)

Directed by David Anspaugh.

Starring Gene Hackman, Barbara Hershey, Dennis Hopper.

THE SHORT STORY ★ Set in the '50s, this is a story about championship basketball before the NBA hotshots started making big bucks. We're talking high-school hoops here. But to the people of small-town Indiana, the game means everything. Gene Hackman plays a washed-up coach looking for a second chance. Watch for Dennis Hopper as the town basketball fanatic with an alcohol problem. Just when you think you have a handle on things, this turns out to be a movie about redemption.

MEMORABLE LINE ★ A local's take on the new coach: "A man who comes to a place like this, either he's runnin' away from something or he has nowhere else to go."

MESSAGE ★ Everyone deserves another chance to shine.

Ice Castles (1979)

Directed by Donald Wrye.

Starring Lynn-Holly Johnson, Robby Benson, Colleen Dewhurst.

THE SHORT STORY ★ A solid cast avoid gooey sentiment in this surprisingly effective story of an accomplished female ice skater who's blinded in a freak accident. The skating sequences make this one especially worthwhile, although romance is the main attraction. Don't be surprised if you need your hanky for this one. It has a way of getting to you.

MEMORABLE MOMENT ★ Any time we see a skating sequence.

MESSAGE ★ Keep doing what you love.

CHECK THIS OUT ★ If hockey is more your style, try 1977's *Slap Shot*.

Kitchen Party (1997)

Written and directed by Gary Burns.

Starring Scott Speedman, Tygh Runyan, Jessica Leis.

THE SHORT STORY ★ Scott decides to throw a party while his parents are out for the evening. The catch? He promises his clean-freak mom he'll confine the gathering to the kitchen. The clever premise shifts between the parents' dreary cocktail party and the awkward socializing at Scott's. You keep expecting this to degenerate into absolute silliness. Instead, we're treated to a darkly funny look at teen angst. Speedman has real presence as Scott. But the rest of the cast does a great job as well.

MEMORABLE MOMENT ★ The beer scene.

MESSAGE ★ Even when you win, you lose.

Following in their footsteps

Keifer Sutherland (*Flatliners, Lost Boys*) is the son of actor **Donald Sutherland** (*M*A*S*H*). Oscar-winning actress **Gywneth Paltrow** (*Shakespeare in Love*) is the daughter of *The Great Santini's* **Blythe Danner**. **Jennifer Jason Leigh** (*Single White Female, Fast Times at Ridgemont High*) is the daughter of actor **Vic Morrow** (*Twilight Zone, Blackboard Jungle*).

Jamie Leigh Curtis (*Trading Places*) is the daughter of **Janet Leigh** (*Psycho*) and **Tony Curtis** (*Some Like It Hot*). **Kate Hudson** (*Almost Famous*) is the daughter of **Goldie Hawn** (*Private Benjamin*). **Drew Barrymore** (*E.T., Ever After*) is the youngest in a long line of distinguished actors that include **John, Ethel, and Lionel Barrymore**.

Lucas (1986)

Written and directed by David Seltzer.

Starring Corey Haim, Kerri Green, Charlie Sheen.

THE SHORT STORY ★ The life of a pint-sized 14-year-old nerd has seldom been so accurately or so lovingly portrayed. Corey Haim's Lucas is so smart that he's managed to skip ahead in school. Unfortunately, he seems years behind his peers in every area except brains. And brains aren't everything when it comes to falling in love with a young woman a full two years older.

MEMORABLE MOMENT ★ Lucas in football shoulder pads.

MESSAGE ★ If you hang in there long enough, something's bound to change.

Mr. Holland's Opus (1995)

Directed by Stephen Herek.

Starring Richard Dreyfuss, Glenne Headly, Olympia Dukakis.

THE SHORT STORY ★ The story of a dedicated music teacher who throws himself into his work at the expense of his personal life. Richard Dreyfuss injects the title role with energy and affection. Anyone who's ever played an instrument in the school band should catch this one.

MEMORABLE LINE ★ Mr. Holland's philosophy: "Playing music is supposed to be fun. It's about heart, it's about feelings … It's not about the notes."

MESSAGE ★ Teaching is worth it.

CHECK THIS OUT ★ For another movie about an inspirational teacher, catch 1987's *Stand and Deliver*.

My American Cousin (1985)

Written and directed by Sandy Wilson.

Starring Margaret Langrick, John Wildman, Richard Donat.

THE SHORT STORY ★ It's the summer of 1959. Margaret Langrick stars as Sandy Wilcox, a bored teen living in a small British Columbia town where—as she writes in her diary—"nothing ever happens." All that changes when Sandy's older American cousin breezes in at the wheel of a red Cadillac convertible. As cousin Butch, John Wildman is the epitome of '50s teenaged cool. Sandy can't imagine anybody having a more carefree life. But everything isn't quite as it seems.

MEMORABLE LINE ★ Sandy quoting the philosophy of her mother: "Boys are like buses. You miss one, another will be along shortly."

MESSAGE ★ Given the right time and place, a special person can change your life.

CHECK THIS OUT ★ For another memorable trip into the '50s, try 1973's *American Graffiti*.

My Bodyguard (1980)

Directed by Tony Bill.

Starring Chris Makepeace, Adam Baldwin, Ruth Gordon.

THE SHORT STORY ★ A kid is getting bullied at school. His solution? Hook up with the big, sullen loner everyone else is too scared to hang around with. One of my favorite coming-of-age films. Just when you think it will keep happily skimming the surface, it insists on digging deeper. If you've ever been picked on, this is a movie you'll definitely relate to. Chris Makepeace gives the performance of his career.

MEMORABLE MOMENT ★ The motorbike ride.

MESSAGE ★ Some good can come out of misery when you least expect it.

CHECK THIS OUT ★ *My Bodyguard*'s Ruth Gordon gives the performance of her career in 1972's darkly bizarre *Harold and Maude*.

My Brilliant Career (1979)

Directed by Gillian Armstrong.

Starring Judy Davis, Sam Neill, Wendy Hughes.

Based on the novel by Miles Franklin.

THE SHORT STORY ★ Set in nineteenth-century Australia. Judy Davis makes her debut in the role of Sybylla Melvyn, a determined idealist who dreams of being an author. Refusing to consider marriage despite financial hardship, Sybylla rejects the standard path set out for polite young women of the day. Instead, she chooses to focus on living a life of independence.

MEMORABLE MOMENT ★ The unusual way Sybylla sends off one of her manuscripts to a prospective publisher.

MESSAGE ★ Follow your heart.

My Favorite Year (1982)

Directed by Richard Benjamin.

Starring Peter O'Toole, Mark Linn-Baker, Joseph Bologna.

THE SHORT STORY ★ Set in the '50s, this comedy takes place against the backdrop of live television. A young writer (Linn-Baker) is given the assignment of baby-sitting a troublesome guest star. The legendary Allan Swan is a fading movie idol whose thirst for misadventure is equalled only by his thirst for alcohol. Peter O'Toole is at his comic best as Swann, a washed-up swashbuckler who teaches his young companion a few lessons in life. There's more here than laughs.

MEMORABLE LINE ✶ When Swann hears he's going to be on a live TV broadcast, he explains his stage fright with: "Live? I can't go on live. I'm a movie star not an actor."

MESSAGE ✶ You only go around once.

October Sky (1999)

Directed by Joe Johnston

Starring Jake Gyllenhaal, Chris Cooper, Laura Dern.

Based on the novel by Homer H. Hickham.

THE SHORT STORY ✶ It's the '50s, and everyone has an eye on conquering outer space. Young Homer Hickham dreams of being a rocket scientist, but in a community where the only jobs are in the coal mine, his chances are slim. His one chance is the school science fair. With the encouragement of an understanding teacher, he begins to learn as much as he can about model rocketry. Will Homer succeed in turning around his bleak future? A poignant, subtle tale based on a true story.

MEMORABLE MOMENT ✶ The launching of Homer's first rocket.

MESSAGE ✶ Reach for the sky.

Pretty in Pink (1986)

Directed by Howard Deutch.

Starring Molly Ringwald, Jon Cryer, Andrew McCarthy.

THE SHORT STORY ✶ Ringwald plays a modern-day Cinderella, a pretty and talented social outcast with an offbeat charm that ends up attracting the attention of a rich hunk (McCarthy). This happens much to the dismay of her nerdy best friend (Cryer), who has an undeclared crush on her. But will the school's snobby rich set accept an outsider? Will our Cinderella live out her high-school fairy tale? There are plenty of twists and turns here, but the ride is well worth it.

MEMORABLE LINE ★ When our heroine tries to convince her rich boyfriend that his money doesn't matter, she blurts, "I'd be happy with you in a Turkish prison!" Is that true love or what?

MESSAGE ★ Sometimes it actually *helps* to believe in fairy tales.

Rocky (1976)

Directed by John G. Avildsen.

Starring Sylvester Stallone, Talia Shire, Burgess Meredith.

THE SHORT STORY ★ Sylvester Stallone stars as Rocky Balboa, a loser with big dreams. This story of a pathetically low-ranked boxer who gets a shot at fighting a champion is one of the ultimate "feel-good" movies of all time. Stallone—who also wrote the screenplay—appeared in no less than four sequels. But none of them have the charm or heart of the original. Great score and a winning performance by Burgess Meredith as Rocky's trainer.

MEMORABLE MOMENT ★ Rocky getting into shape by punching out sides of frozen beef.

MESSAGE ★ Go for it.

Room with a View (1986)

Directed by James Ivory.

Starring Maggie Smith, Helena Bonham Carter, Julian Sands.

Based on the novel by E.M. Forester.

THE SHORT STORY ★ Remember when manners were a form of courtship? No? All the more reason to see this movie. An excellent cast kicks off this tale of romance with a Victorian spin. Nobody says "dude" and everyone knows exactly the right fork to use. But you like them anyway. Set in Florence in the 1900s.

MEMORABLE MOMENT ★ Any conversation around the dinner table.

MESSAGE ★ Young love has been around a long time.

Rudy (1993)

Directed by David Anspaugh.

Starring Sean Astin, Ned Beatty, Robert Prosky.

THE SHORT STORY ★ The inspiring story of a short, small, working-class guy who will stop at nothing to achieve his dream of playing football for Notre Dame. Everybody loves this movie. Rent the video and see why.

MEMORABLE LINE ★ "In this life, you don't have to prove nothin' to nobody but yourself."

MESSAGE ★ Just because you're average doesn't mean you can't be great.

CHECK THIS OUT ★ For another inspiring movie with a football setting, catch Tom Cruise in 1993's *All the Right Moves*.

Making it happen

There are many actors who have also tried their hand at working behind the cameras as directors. The list includes **Tom Hanks** *(That Thing You Do)*, **Tim Robbins** *(Bob Roberts)*, **Kevin Costner** *(Dances With Wolves)*, and **Barbra Streisand** *(Prince of Tides)*.

Say Anything (1989)

Directed by Cameron Crowe.

Starring John Cusack, Ione Skye, John Mahoney.

THE SHORT STORY ★ The devoutly offbeat Lloyd falls in love with high-school valedictorian Diane. It is not a match made in heaven, but they stick it out. Along the way, Diane finds out that her dad isn't the upstanding citizen she thought he was. A thoughtful, funny film about risking it all for the one you love.

MEMORABLE MOMENT ★ When Diane's overprotective dad asks a bumbling Lloyd what he wants to do with his life, he replies that he believes in the future of kick-boxing.

MESSAGE ★ Sometimes love means having to grow up faster than you expected.

Selena (1997)

Directed by Gregory Nava.

Starring Jennifer Lopez, Edward James Olmos, Jon Seda.

THE SHORT STORY ★ The biography of a Latin pop star who met her tragic demise at the hands of a crazed fan. A dark ending doesn't match the rest of this picture about a dynamic singer's rise to the edge of genuine stardom. Jennifer Lopez offers a magnetic and totally confident performance but Olmos nearly steals the picture as her protective father.

MEMORABLE MOMENT ★ When Selena gets mobbed in a department store.

MESSAGE ★ Follow the music.

CHECK THIS OUT ★ For a movie with a similar theme, try 1987's *La Bamba*.

Some Girls (1988)

Directed by Michael Hoffman.

Starring Patrick Dempsey, Jennifer Connelly, Andre Gregory.

THE SHORT STORY ★ A delightfully eccentric little gem about the romantic and social complications that arise when a young man spends Christmas with his girlfriend's family. It may seem slow at first, but hang in there. This one's a keeper.

MEMORABLE MOMENT ★ The naked conversation.

MESSAGE ★ Maybe dating isn't worth it.

Stand By Me (1986)

Directed by Rob Reiner.

Starring Wil Wheaton, River Phoenix, Corey Feldman.

THE SHORT STORY ★ Ever think it would be a good idea to go looking for a corpse? Me neither. But this touching movie could change your mind. The setting is a small town in the '50s. Four buddies are wasting the summer, just hanging out and doing nothing. So when they hear a rumor that a boy has been killed by a train, they set out to find the body. Along the way, they discover more about themselves than they bargained for. While the coarse language doesn't suit the period, this one's still a winner.

MEMORABLE LINE ★ "No, man, seriously. Am I weird?"

MESSAGE ★ Even the simplest journey can take you to unexpected places.

Strictly Ballroom (1992)

Directed by Baz Luhrmann.

Starring Paul Mercurio, Tara Morice, Bill Hunter.

THE SHORT STORY ★ A winning Australian romantic comedy about two mismatched partners who decide to enter a ballroom dance competition. The guy's a great dancer, the girl has two left feet. Wait till you see what happens. If this doesn't make you want to take dance lessons, nothing will.

MEMORABLE MOMENT ★ The first training session.

MESSAGE ★ Sometimes the ugly duckling *can* become a swan.

The Sure Thing (1985)

Directed by Rob Reiner.

Starring John Cusack, Daphne Zuniga, Viveca Lindfors.

THE SHORT STORY ★ A guy embarks on a road trip to hook up with a girl he's been convinced will show him a *really* good time. But he meets someone else who makes him question his plan. This thoughtful, intelligent offering from Rob Reiner is a must see.

MEMORABLE LINE ★ "You're flunking English! That's your mother tongue."

MESSAGE ★ A guy can change his mind.

The World of Henry Orient (1964)

Directed by George Roy Hill.

Starring Peter Sellers, Tippy Walker, Merrie Spaeth.

Based on the novel by Nora Johnson.

THE SHORT STORY ★ Funny, bittersweet story of two teenaged girls who become infatuated with a vain concert pianist played by

Sellers. They proceed to follow him around New York to hilarious effect. It doesn't sound like much of a plot, but this one is a cult classic.

MEMORABLE MOMENT ★ The scene in New York's Central Park.

MESSAGE ★ Enjoy your first crush while you can.

CHECK THIS OUT ★ George Roy Hill also directed another gem about young love, 1979's *A Little Romance*.

Have You Seen These Classics?

Amadeus (1984)

Directed by Milos Forman.

Starring Tom Hulce, F. Murray Abraham, Elizabeth Berridge.

THE SHORT STORY ★ Passion, jealousy, and powdered wigs. There's some pretty decent music in here, too. This lush period piece about young Wolfgang Amadeus Mozart and his rivalry with a fellow composer won multiple Oscars in addition to best picture. Tom Hulce plays the self-indulgent musical genius like the world's first rock star. This movie's long, but it's an elegant change of pace from the usual "Hey, let's start a band!" picture.

MEMORABLE LINE ★ Musical rival Salieri on hearing Mozart's work for the first time: "This was music I'd never heard before. It seemed to be the voice of God."

MESSAGE ★ You don't have to be nice just because you're a genius.

Casablanca (1942)

Directed by Michael Curtiz.

Starring Humphrey Bogart, Ingrid Bergman, Claude Rains.

THE SHORT STORY ★ Your cinematic education isn't complete without this one. Rick is a cynical loner who runs a nightclub in Morocco during World War II. His life changes when he agrees to help an old flame and her husband with a dangerous problem. It's packed with intrigue, romance, and great performances. But this is really a story about a man deciding to do the right thing. You'll want to see Casablanca more than once. Like the man said, "This could be the beginning of a beautiful friendship."

MEMORABLE LINE ★ "We'll always have Paris."

MESSAGE ★ There are times when loving someone means leaving them behind.

The Godfather: Part II (1974)

Directed by Francis Ford Coppola.

Starring Al Pacino, Robert De Niro, Diane Keaton.

THE SHORT STORY ★ This just may be the best sequel ever made. The first *Godfather* has a stunning performance by Marlon Brando as Vito Corleone, an aging Mafia don. But this Oscar-winning follow-up goes back further to trace the roots of the crime family. A fascinating study of a young man on the road to corruption and beyond.

MEMORABLE LINE ★ "This is the business we chose."

MESSAGE ★ Power corrupts.

CHECK THIS OUT ★ Rent 1971's *The Godfather*. Warning: *The Godfather: Part III* (1990) is for die-hard fans only.

Great Expectations (1946)

Directed by David Lean.

Starring John Mills, Valerie Hobson, Bernard Miles.

Based on the novel by Charles Dickens.

THE SHORT STORY ★ This classic about a poor orphan whose luck changes for the better gets the David Lean treatment. This is an exquisite example of how a great book can become a great movie without missing a beat. There are other versions out there but none of them comes close to this one.

MEMORABLE MOMENT ★ The graveyard scene.

MESSAGE ★ Never underestimate the power of fate.

CHECK THIS OUT ★ George Cukor's 1935 version of another Dickens novel, *David Copperfield*.

Jane Eyre (1944)

Directed by Robert Stevenson.

Starring Orson Welles, Joan Fontaine.

THE SHORT STORY ★ Dark, moody, and completely captivating screen adaptation of the Charlotte Brontë novel about an orphan girl who becomes a governess in a mysterious mansion, only to discover some unexpected complications. Orson Welles plays the brooding Rochester to perfection.

MEMORABLE MOMENT ★ When Jane first meets Rochester.

MESSAGE ★ Life can lead you to some strange and wonderful places.

CHECK THIS OUT ★ Franco Zeffirelli's 1996 version of *Jane Eyre* with Willam Hurt and Charlotte Gainsbourg.

My Fair Lady (1964)

Directed by George Cukor.

Starring Audrey Hepburn, Rex Harrison, Stanley Holloway.

THE SHORT STORY ★ The film version of the smash Broadway musical, based on George Bernard Shaw's play *Pygmalion*. Rex Harrison plays a stuffy elocution professor who attempts to transform a Cockney flower seller into a lady. Audrey Hepburn's Eliza Doolittle is co-operative—to a point. This classic battle of wills is set to the beat of a delightful Lerner and Lowe score. Hepburn's singing voice is dubbed by another artist. But who cares? She's still Audrey Hepburn.

MEMORABLE LINE ★ "Why can't the English learn to *speak?*"

MESSAGE ★ Be true to yourself.

CHECK THIS OUT ★ 1938's *Pygmalion* with Wendy Hiller as Eliza.

The Prime of Miss Jean Brodie (1969)

Directed by Ronald Neame.

Starring Maggie Smith, Robert Stephens, Pamela Franklin.

Based on the novel by Muriel Spark.

THE SHORT STORY ★ A fascinating character study of an unconventional teacher at a Scottish girls' school who has a mesmerizing effect on her students. As Jean Brodie, Oscar-winner Maggie Smith gives the finest performance of her long and distinguished career. A thought-provoking story that questions just how far a teacher should go when it comes to influencing young minds.

MEMORABLE LINE ★ Miss Brody's philosophy? "Give me a girl at an impressionable age and she is mine for life."

MESSAGE ★ Sometimes, the person you trust most is the one who is taking greatest advantage of you.

Red River (1948)

Directed by Howard Hawks.

Starring John Wayne, Montgomery Clift, Walter Brennan.

THE SHORT STORY ★ Set against the backdrop of a cattle drive along the Chisholm Trail in 1865, this vintage cowboy drama centers on the struggle of a young man to understand his tyrannical trail boss. Montgomery Clift makes his film debut as the sensitive Matthew Garth. John Wayne plays the tough-as-nails Thomas Dunson, Garth's boss and guardian. Wayne's portrayal is one of the best in his long career. Worth catching for one of the most surprising "fight scenes" in any Western.

MEMORABLE LINE ★ A defiant Matthew to Dunson. "Don't tell me what to think. I'll take your orders about work but not about what to think."

MESSAGE ★ The road to adulthood can be rougher than moving ten thousand head of cattle.

Tom Jones (1963)

Directed by Tony Richardson.

Starring Albert Finney, Susannah York, Hugh Griffith.

Based on the novel by Henry Fielding.

THE SHORT STORY ★ A young man coming of age in eighteenth-century England is determined to make the most of his life. The movie is a happy, bawdy romp that's lost none of its charm over the decades. Few films have managed to communicate the joy of youth and independence with such complete success.

MEMORABLE MOMENT ★ The dining scene.

MESSAGE ★ You're only young once.

West Side Story (1961)

Directed by Robert Wise, Jerome Robbins.

Starring Natalie Wood, Richard Beymer, Rita Moreno.

THE SHORT STORY ★ The film adaptation of the hit Broadway musical about two rival street gangs is based on Shakespeare's *Romeo and Juliet*. Passionate performances and a timeless score combine for a genuinely moving experience. They don't make them like this any more. Music and lyrics by Leonard Bernstein and Stephen Sondheim. Winner of ten Oscars, including best picture.

MEMORABLE MOMENT ★ Pick a song. Any song.

MESSAGE ★ Love can be dangerous.

Making an impact

Filmmaker **John Hughes** *(The Breakfast Club, Ferris Bueller's Day Off)* started off as a writer for the humor magazine *National Lampoon*. When he was 16, he visited a Zen temple and was kicked out for making noise. Of the teen years, he has said: "At that age, it feels as good to feel bad as it does to feel good."

As prolific a writer as he is fast, Hughes reportedly penned the scripts for *The Breakfast Club* and *Weird Science* in a total time of two days each. He is especially gratified by *The Breakfast Club*, saying: "I'm proud that it has lasted … It's really about characters and what they have to say."

The Great Escape

★ ★ ★ ★ ★

Sometimes you just need to escape the real world for a while, and these movies will help you do just that. This category includes action films, adventure movies and romance. With a couple of exceptions, there's nothing too heavy or serious here—just a chance to travel to outer space, the Australian outback or the Old West, to test your mettle with engaging characters like Crocodile Dundee or Indiana Jones, or to swoon over the romantic complications of *Much Ado About Nothing*.

Blade Runner (1982)

Directed by Ridley Scott.

Starring Harrison Ford, Rutger Hauer, Sean Young.

THE SHORT STORY ★ The sci-fi setting is Los Angeles, 2019. Bounty hunter Rick Deckard (Ford) is on a mission to destroy a dangerous gang of renegade "replicants." These humanlike androids, created for the convenience of others, are now rebelling against their masters. Led by the highly intelligent android Roy Batty, they are desperate to increase their limited lifespans. Will Deckard survive long enough to discover why these androids insist on clinging to life?

MEMORABLE LINE ★ Batty trying to explain to Deckard why he wants to keep living: "I've seen things you people wouldn't believe … All those … moments will be lost in time like tears in the rain."

MESSAGE ★ Sometimes, you find humanity where you least expect it.

Braveheart (1995)

Directed by Mel Gibson.

Starring Mel Gibson, Sophie Marceau, Patrick McGoohan.

THE SHORT STORY ★ A rollercoaster ride through a fascinating period in history. This Best Picture winner stars actor-director Gibson as William Wallace, a thirteenth-century Scottish rebel who wages war against the tyranny of English rule. It's a true epic in every way. You get scope, size, and a rousing adventure that stirs the blood. At the same time, the film has an intimacy that's missing in many blockbusters, because it celebrates the spirit of the individual.

MEMORABLE MOMENT ★ Any battle scene.

MESSAGE ★ Some things are worth dying for.

CHECK THIS OUT ★ For another historical adventure with a Scottish setting, catch 1995's *Rob Roy*.

Brazil (1985)

Directed by Terry Gilliam.

Starring Jonathan Pryce, Kim Greist, Robert De Niro.

THE SHORT STORY ★ This futuristic tale of a bleak world focuses on the frustrations of a mild-mannered clerk (Pryce) as he tries to correct an error in paperwork. It's a dark satire that has often been compared to George Orwell's famous novel, *1984,* but this movie provides a few more laughs. Director Terry Gilliam creates a fascinating backdrop for a fresh examination of the human condition. This movie is long and over-reaching. But I'll take that kind of ambition over something that plays it safe.

MEMORABLE MOMENT ★ The face-stretching scene.

MESSAGE ★ Everybody needs an escape from the mundane.

Taking a chance

At 15, **Sylvester Stallone**'s classmates voted him "most likely to end up in the electric chair." But the tough guy had other plans. As a struggling actor, he penned the script for *Rocky.* Hollywood was interested in the screenplay but Stallone refused to sell it unless they allowed him to play the lead. It was a huge risk but it paid off and made him a major star.

Butch Cassidy and the Sundance Kid (1969)

Directed by George Roy Hill.

Starring Paul Newman, Robert Redford, Katharine Ross.

THE SHORT STORY ★ In this light-hearted Western, Butch Cassidy and the Sundance Kid are two notorious outlaws who seem to care as much about friendship and good times as they do about robbing banks. Loosely based on a true story, this tale of changing times in the Old West has a distinctly modern feel. As Butch and Sundance, Newman and Redford play two of the most likeable crooks in movie history. This has my vote for the ultimate "buddy film."

MEMORABLE LINE ★ Pursued by a relentless "superposse," Butch and Sundance find themselves at the edge of a high cliff. Their only means of escape is to dive into a stream far below. A reluctant Sundance confesses that he can't swim. The highly amused Butch laughs, "The *fall'll* probably kill ya!"

MESSAGE ★ If you're going to be an outlaw, you might as well have fun doing it.

Close Encounters of the Third Kind (1977)

Written and directed by Steven Spielberg.

Starring Richard Dreyfuss, François Truffaut, Teri Garr.

THE SHORT STORY ★ This is required viewing for anyone who's ever fantasized about taking off in a flying saucer. If not *the* best film ever made about an alien encounter, it's certainly one of the most comforting. Rent the video and see what I mean. Richard Dreyfuss has never been more suited to a role. A great score by John Williams, and special effects that will take your breath away. If you get a chance to experience this on the big screen, jump at it.

MEMORABLE MOMENT ★ The first time you hear those five notes chime.

MESSAGE ★ Why not?

Crocodile Dundee (1986)

Directed by Peter Faiman.

Starring Paul Hogan, Linda Koslowski, John Meillon.

THE SHORT STORY ★ Paul Hogan stars in the title role as a charming Australian wilderness guide wise in the ways of the outback. He introduces an attractive visiting American reporter, Sue Charlton, to his natural surroundings. But the fun really starts when Dundee follows Sue back to her native urban jungle of New York City. The huge success of this movie inspired two less successful sequels.

MEMORABLE LINE ★ When Dundee encounters a New York thug brandishing a switchblade, he pulls out his own large hunting knife. "That's a knife," he says.

MESSAGE ★ You can take the guy out of the outback but you can't take the outback out of the guy.

Deeply (2000)

Written and directed by Sheri Elwood.

Starring Kirsten Dunst, Lynn Redgrave, Brent Carver.

THE SHORT STORY ★ The plight of an unhappy young woman is beautifully interwoven with a bittersweet fable of a girl intent on saving her small fishing village from certain disaster. Lynn

Redgrave plays the storyteller who pulls it all together. *Deeply* takes a while to build, but this romantic spin on an ancient curse is well worth the wait. Kirsten Dunst is wonderful as a feisty, pipe-smoker who definitely knows her own mind.

MEMORABLE MOMENT ★ The tent scene on the beach.

MESSAGE ★ Believe in the power of a good story.

The price of fame

As a child growing up in China, **Jackie Chan** *(Rush Hour)* was trained in dance, music and the martial arts. His comic style has been influenced by his admiration of such silent film giants as **Buster Keaton** and **Harold Lloyd**. He reportedly earned more than $15 million for *Rush Hour 2*. But he works *hard* for his money. Chan's fearless stunt work has resulted in three broken noses, a broken ankle and two broken cheekbones. "Don't try to be like Jackie," he has said. "Study computers instead."

The Dove (1974)

Directed by Charles Jarrot.

Starring Joseph Bottoms, Deborah Raffin, Dabney Coleman.

THE SHORT STORY ★ The hardships and pleasures one young man experiences when he decides to sail around the world on his own at the age of 16. Beautifully photographed and an inspiration to anyone who's ever considered facing the sea alone. The title comes from the name of the sailboat. Based on a true story.

MEMORABLE MOMENT ★ Any time the *Dove* is out on the water.

MESSAGE ★ You don't know what you can do until you try.

Edward Scissorhands (1990)

Directed by Tim Burton.

Starring Johnny Depp, Winona Ryder, Dianne Weist.

THE SHORT STORY ✭ Quirky fable about a gentle android whose creator dies before giving the android real hands. The uneven tone of this movie can't mar Tim Burton's highly original vision. Watch for horror movie great Vincent Price in one of his last roles.

MEMORABLE MOMENT ✭ Watching Edward cut anything.

MESSAGE ✭ It's not easy being different

Ever After (1998)

Directed by Andy Tennant.

Starring Drew Barrymore, Angelica Huston, Dougray Scott.

THE SHORT STORY ✭ Want a princess who rolls up her sleeves and gets the job done? Drew Barrymore shines in a clever version of *Cinderella* that dusts off the old attitudes and adds a welcome spark of feminism. You'll never look at fairy tales the same way again. Angelica Huston is a big, wicked plus.

MEMORABLE LINE ✭ "A life without love is no life at all."

MESSAGE ✭ Living happily ever after is hard work. But somebody's got to do it.

CHECK THIS OUT ✭ To see more of Drew, try 1993's *The Wedding Singer*.

Far from Home: The Adventures of Yellow Dog (1995)

Written and directed by Philip Borsos.

Starring Jesse Bradford, Mimi Rogers, Bruce Davison.

THE SHORT STORY ★ After a boating accident, young Angus McCormick is stranded in the British Columbian wilderness with only his dog Yellow for comfort and support. With little in the manner of tools or provisions, the friends find their resourcefulness pushed to the limit. This is a quiet, majestic movie that isn't afraid to unfold slowly. Along the way, it says much about the beauty and power of nature. Jesse Bradford gives a strong performance as Angus.

MEMORABLE MOMENT ★ When Angus's dad inherits his dad's old pocket knife.

MESSAGE ★ Sometimes you have to get lost in order to find yourself

CHECK THIS OUT ★ Jesse Bradford also does a great job in the critically acclaimed *King of the Hill* (1993).

Field of Dreams (1989)

Directed by Phil Robinson.

Starring Kevin Costner, Amy Madigan, James Earl Jones.

Based on the novel *Shoeless Joe* by W.P. Kinsella.

THE SHORT STORY ★ One of the best movies ever made about believing in magic when others tell you not to. A dreamer hears voices that inspire him to construct a baseball diamond in his Iowa cornfield. This act of faith results in the ghosts of various ballplayers arriving to pay homage. But that doesn't even begin to describe what happens here. See the film and be encouraged to ignore common sense for all the right reasons.

MEMORABLE LINE ★ "If you build it, they will come."

MESSAGE ★ Faith can make a miracle happen.

Fly Away Home (1996)

Directed by Carroll Ballard.

Starring Jeff Daniels, Anna Paquin, Dana Delany.

THE SHORT STORY ★ Recovering from the death of her mother, a girl is forced to move to Canada and live with a father she barely knows. The situation is tense until the girl decides to raise a flock of orphaned baby geese. Father and daughter are brought closer when they discover one important fact of nature: it's up to the two of them to teach the geese to migrate. This is a real gem, warm-hearted but never sappy. Paquin is a delight as an emotionally fragile girl who finds solace in the act of nurturing.

MEMORABLE MOMENT ★ The patterning scene.

MESSAGE ★ There's more than one way to fly.

Gladiator (2000)

Directed by Ridley Scott.

Starring Russell Crowe, Joaquin Phoenix, Richard Harris.

THE SHORT STORY ★ Set in ancient Rome, *Gladiator* tells the story of a slave who wins the respect of the public through his consummate skill in the arena. No great surprise, really, since he's an honored soldier whose fortunes changed when he refused to transfer his allegiance to the new emperor. Russell Crowe endows the title role with empathy and intelligence. Dazzling special effects and a top-notch supporting cast helped win an

Oscar for best picture. Spectacle to spare.

MEMORABLE MOMENT ★ Any of the fight scenes.

MESSAGE ★ Freedom starts from within.

CHECK THIS OUT ★ For a classic take on the gladiator movie, watch 1960's *Spartacus*.

Good Morning, Vietnam (1987)
Directed by Barry Levinson.

Starring Robin Williams, Forest Whitaker, Bruno Kirby.

THE SHORT STORY ★ The setting is Vietnam in 1965. American DJ Adrian Cronauer (Williams) is stationed in Saigon and working for Armed Forces Radio. His conservative military bosses want him to keep the music and the patter tame. But Cronauer—whose audience consists of young soldiers eager for rock 'n' roll—wants to keep things wild and crazy. Robin Williams gives a sensitive performance as a nice guy striving to understand a different culture. But what you'll really appreciate are his hilarious antics behind the mike.

MEMORABLE LINE ★ Cronauer's signature bellow: "Good mor-ning Viet-nam!"

MESSAGE ★ Stick up for what you believe in.

CHECK THIS OUT ★ For the story of another unusual DJ, try 1990's *Pump Up the Volume*.

Gorillas in the Mist (1988)
Directed by Michael Apted.

Starring Sigourney Weaver, Bryan Brown, Julie Harris.

THE SHORT STORY ★ Unique dramatization based on the life of Dian Fossey, a researcher who dedicated her career to understanding the behavior patterns of the African mountain gorilla. This film works as an empathetic study of a fascinating species but it also manages to weave in elements of suspense and adventure. Sigourney Weaver is captivating as the complex Fossey. Discover this one for yourself.

MEMORABLE MOMENT ★ When Fossey begins interaction with the gorillas.

MESSAGE ★ Animals are more like us than we think.

CHECK THIS OUT ★ For another spin on primates, catch 1987's *Project X*.

Climbing the ladder

Before getting a break as the lead in *Selena*, one of **Jennifer Lopez**'s early jobs in show business was as a dancer on TV's "In Living Color." In addition to a thriving musical career, she is the highest-paid Latin American actress in the movies, receiving a reported $9 million for her role in *The Wedding Planner*.

Grease (1978)

Directed by Randal Kleiser.

Starring John Travolta, Olivia Newton-John, Stockard Channing.

THE SHORT STORY ★ Can a cool greaser find happiness with a sweet girl? The '50s were never really like this. But who cares? This high-energy musical never goes out of style. Packed with great numbers and a cast who really seem to be enjoying themselves. See it again. You know you want to.

MEMORABLE MOMENT ✱ Any musical number.

MESSAGE ✱ True love really does conquer all. Especially when you can dance.

Harry Potter and the Sorcerer's Stone (2001)

Directed by Chris Columbus.

Starring Daniel Radcliffe, Robbie Coltrane, Maggie Smith.

Based on the novel by J.K. Rowling.

THE SHORT STORY ✱ Let's face it. You have to be almost as resourceful as Harry Potter himself to adapt a J.K. Rowling book for the big screen. Director Chris Columbus pulls off the trick with surprising skill. Sure, there are going to be a few whiners— aren't there always?—but this universally adored story of a boy learning the ins and outs of witchcraft will satisfy the large majority of ardent fans. Besides, there'll be enough sequels in the immediate future to cut everyone some slack.

MEMORABLE MOMENT ✱ The arrival of a letter that will change Harry's life.

MESSAGE ✱ Magic rules!

A League of their Own (1992)

Directed by Penny Marshall.

Starring Tom Hanks, Geena Davis, Madonna.

THE SHORT STORY ✱ This story of a World War II baseball league composed entirely of women players has much to recommend it. For one thing, it's refreshing to see women playing sports on the screen for a change. But this is really a story about the friendships that form through teamwork. Tom Hanks is just right as an over-the-hill player turned coach, but it's the largely female cast that puts the pepper in this movie. Madonna proves once again that she can act as well as sing.

MEMORABLE LINE ★ When a player breaks out in tears, the manager reminds his team, "There's no crying in baseball."

MESSAGE ★ Play ball.

Early start

Drew Barrymore made her feature-film debut at the age of 4. At 7, she was the youngest person to host *Saturday Night Live*. When she was 14, she co-wrote her autobiography, *Little Girl Lost*.

Little Women (1994)

Directed by Gillian Armstrong.

Starring Winona Ryder, Susan Sarandon, Trina Alvarado.

Based on the novel by Louisa May Alcott.

THE SHORT STORY ★ This is a marvellous adaptation with a cast that's hard to beat. It's also the fourth attempt at bringing the book to life on screen. So what makes this timeless tale of four devoted sisters so watchable? The chemistry between the players. Everyone is just great here. But pay close attention to veteran character actor Mary Wickes, who's having the time of her life playing a sour aunt.

MEMORABLE LINE ★ "I could never love anyone as I love my sisters."

MESSAGE ★ There's nothing like togetherness.

CHECK THIS OUT ★ George Cukor's 1933 version of *Little Women* starring Katharine Hepburn.

Lord of the Rings: The Fellowship of the Ring (2001)

Directed by Peter Jackson.

Starring Elijah Wood, Sean Astin, Ian McKellen.

Based on the novel by J.R.R. Tolkien.

THE SHORT STORY ★ Since there's a fair amount of the book—written as a trilogy—that didn't make it to the screen, this adaptation of Tolkien's epic fantasy may not satisfy fanatical purists. But having said that, this tale of a resourceful young Hobbit entrusted with an ancient Ring is an affectionate, faithful rendering that relies on a lot more than impressive special effects. There are at least two sequels on the way in short order. Since the films were shot simultaneously, we'll get to see the same excellent cast throughout.

MEMORABLE MOMENT ★ Take your pick of the battle scenes.

MESSAGE ★ Power can come in small packages.

Mad Max II: The Road Warrior (1981)

Directed by George Miller.

Starring Mel Gibson, Bruce Spence, Vernon Wells.

THE SHORT STORY ★ A highly original futuristic actioneer. Set in a post-apocalyptic wasteland where gasoline is invaluable, this sequel to *Mad Max* is the superior movie stunt-wise. But you won't hear me complaining about either movie. Rent both and see why Mel Gibson became a major star. While you're at it, be thankful we don't have to live in the world it portrays.

MEMORABLE LINE ★ "I got a recipe for snake. Delicious …"

MESSAGE ★ We don't need another hero. This one will do.

CHECK THIS OUT ★ 1985's *Mad Max Beyond Thunderdome*.

The Mask (1994)

Directed by Chuck Russell.

Starring Jim Carrey, Cameron Diaz, Peter Riegert.

THE SHORT STORY ★ This is the closest you'll ever come to seeing a human cartoon. Jim Carrey stars as a meek clerk in desperate need of a personality transplant. He gets one after discovering a mask that transforms him into an aggressively lurid, "out there" guy. His mission? He wants to be more than obnoxious. A frantic pace and novel special effects make this movie pretty impressive, especially the first time around. Think of it as a comic book with the pages flipping really fast.

MEMORABLE LINE ★ "Somebody stop me!"

MESSAGE ★ It's not easy being green.

The Matrix (1999)

Directed by the Wachowski Brothers.

Starring Keanu Reeves, Laurence Fishburne, Carrie-Anne Moss.

THE SHORT STORY ★ Is it possible to overstate how glorious the special effects are here? I don't *think* so. The story can be kind of hard to follow. But any project that blends state-of-the art movie magic with martial arts and hacker lore can throw a few curves my way any time. This is a franchise that should keep going for a while. So enjoy. And remember, don't try this stuff at home.

MEMORABLE MOMENT ★ The fight scenes.

MESSAGE ★ Computers are fine but we still need people to take care of business.

A Midsummer Night's Dream (1999)

Directed by Michael Hoffman.

Starring Kevin Kline, Michelle Pfeiffer, Stanley Tucci.

THE SHORT STORY ★ This totally charming version of Shakespeare's delightfully mixed-up romance is set in nineteenth-century Italy. In this classic tale, fairies work their confounding magic on unsuspecting humans. The perfect cast includes Stanley Tucci as the mischievous Puck, Kevin Kline as Bottom, and Michelle Pfeiffer as a luminous Titania.

MEMORABLE MOMENT ★ Tucci's Puck on a vintage bicycle.

MESSAGE ★ What fools these mortals be.

Much Ado About Nothing (1993)

Directed by Kenneth Branagh.

Starring Kenneth Branagh, Emma Thompson, Denzel Washington.

THE SHORT STORY ★ As Beatrice and Benedict, Branagh and Thompson exchange barbs faster than Jackie Chan can kick you where it hurts. A sunny, light-hearted romance courtesy of Shakespeare. The Tuscan setting bathes the cast in sunlight—no wonder they're so alive with good humor. If this doesn't turn you on to the Bard, you deserve to fall asleep in English class.

MESSAGE ★ The opposite of love isn't hate. It's indifference.

CHECK THIS OUT ★ If romance is not your style try Kenneth Branagh's 1989 version of Shakespeare's *Henry V.*

Pleasantville (1998)

Written and directed by Gary Ross.

Starring Jeff Daniels, Joan Allen, Tobey Maguire.

THE SHORT STORY ★ A brother and sister are magically introduced to the simpler times of a '50s TV sitcom. Everything is peachy in the black-and-white Pleasantville until the two begin to stir things up with their contemporary ideas. The ambitious concept is not all fun and games. But it's easy to forgive this clever movie for stretching things a little too thin. Look for *The Andy Griffith Show*'s Don Knotts in his best role since the bumbling Barney Fife.

MEMORABLE MOMENT ★ The changing colors.

MESSAGE ★ Nothing is ever perfect.

CHECK THIS OUT ★ Jeff Daniels plays a movie character come to life in 1985's *The Purple Rose of Cairo*.

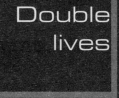

Double lives

Men in Black's **Will Smith** not only acts, he also has a successful career as a hip-hop artist. In 1989, he won the first Grammy award for Best Rap Performance for the song "Parents Just Don't Understand."

The Princess Bride (1987)

Directed by Rob Reiner.

Starring Cary Elwes, Mandy Patinkin, Robin Wright.

Based on the novel by William Goldman.

THE SHORT STORY ★ Swordplay, magic, and much more. The perfect bedtime story, even if you've long since outgrown the practice. This is what happened in fairy tales before your parents decided to cut out the good parts. Funny, charming, and wickedly fast. William Goldman won an Oscar for the screenplay. Try it, you'll like it.

MEMORABLE LINE ★ "My name is Inigo Montoya. You killed my father. Prepare to die."

MESSAGE ★ There's more to fairy tales than you might imagine.

The Rocketeer (1991)

Directed by Joe Johnston.

Starring Bill Campbell, Jennifer Connelly, Alan Arkin.

THE SHORT STORY ★ This affectionate attempt to revive an old-fashioned action-adventure succeeds with style. In a story set in the '30s, Bill Campbell plays a pilot who discovers a rocket pack that turns him into a jet-propelled hero. Not surprisingly, the secret weapon is much in demand. Timothy Dalton has fun chewing up the scenery as an oily bad guy. The rest of the cast underplays with sweet conviction.

MEMORABLE MOMENT ★ Testing the rocket pack.

MESSAGE ★ Who needs an airplane?

The Rocky Horror Picture Show (1975)

Directed by Jim Sharman.

Starring Susan Sarandon, Barry Bostwick, Tim Curry.

THE SHORT STORY ★ A cult favorite. Be warned: this *very* strange musical horror spoof isn't for everyone. Most people get to it eventually through word of mouth. An infectious musical score combines with seriously outrageous characters for what may be an acquired taste. But why not try to surrender to its loopy charm? Whatever you feel about this movie, it scores big points for originality. Avoid the sequel, which is just plain bad.

MEMORABLE MOMENT ★ The Time Warp.

MESSAGE ★ If your car breaks down on a dark and stormy night, maybe it's better to just lock the doors and stay inside.

Repeat success

Several of the movies in this category have found a home on the small screen as TV series. While *Star Trek* started as a popular TV series, *The Young Indiana Jones Chronicles* and the short-lived sitcom *A League of the Own*—featuring director **Rob Reiner's** daughter Tracy—were spun off from the big screen. The characters of Sherlock Holmes, Robin Hood, and Shane have also featured in TV series.

Roxanne (1987)

Directed by Fred Schepisi.

Starring Steve Martin, Daryl Hannah, Rick Rossovich.

THE SHORT STORY ★ Steve Martin stars as C.D. Bales in this comic update of *Cyrano de Bergerac*. The shy and sensitive Bales is a great guy in every way. The only thing that sets him up for ridicule is his *huge* nose. He has a crush on the beautiful Roxanne (Hannah) but so does his pal, the handsome but socially inept Chris (Rossovich). C.D. agrees to secretly help his friend win Roxanne's heart. With Bales pulling the romantic strings in the background, Roxanne falls for Chris. But who is she really falling for?

MEMORABLE LINE ★ While reeling off a series of twenty clever insults regarding the size of his nose, C.D. includes this one. "Uh, would you mind not bobbing your head. The orchestra keeps changing tempo."

MESSAGE ★ Looks aren't even *close* to being everything.

Rush Hour (1998)

Directed by Brent Ratner.

Starring Jackie Chan, Chris Tucker.

THE SHORT STORY ★ What a ride! Jackie Chan has been called a cross between comedy great Buster Keaton and Bruce Lee. Translation? If you like lightning-quick martial arts mixed in with a little slapstick, Jackie's your man. This movie has a standard plot involving a Hong Kong cop who travels to L.A. to help out a friend. Sure, it's predictable, but Chan works so hard to keep us entertained, we'll forgive him.

MEMORABLE MOMENT ★ Any time Jackie breaks into a move.

MESSAGE ★ Move out of the way before somebody gets hurt.

CHECK THIS OUT ★ 2001's *Rush Hour 2*.

The Seven Percent Solution (1976)

Directed by Herbert Ross.

Starring Nicol Williamson, Robert Duvall, Vanessa Redgrave.

Based on the book by Nicholas Meyer.

THE SHORT STORY ✶ Are you a fan of Sherlock Holmes? Well, the usual game's afoot, but the path's a little different this time. Holmes travels to Vienna to get help with his cocaine addiction from none other than the famous psychiatrist Sigmund Freud. This is my favorite Holmes movie of them all. Robert Duvall plays Watson like the intelligent sidekick he was always meant to be. This is a wonderful homage to the legacy of Holmes's creator Arthur Conan Doyle.

MEMORABLE MOMENT ✶ The tennis match.

MESSAGE ✶ There are some problems you can't solve by yourself.

Shakespeare in Love (1998)

Directed by John Madden.

Starring Joseph Fiennes, Gwyneth Paltrow, Geoffrey Rush.

THE SHORT STORY ✶ A vividly realized comedy that blows the dust off Shakespeare by showing him as a struggling young writer in the grip of romance. This should be compulsory viewing for anyone who takes the Bard's plays a little *too* seriously. It's not only a clever conceit, it's also a vivid recreation of Shakespeare's time and place. If things seem a little relaxed, this movie is all the better for it. Oscar winner for best picture.

MEMORABLE MOMENT ✶ Shakespeare struggling to write a little thing called *Romeo and Juliet*.

MESSAGE ✶ Even a master playwright can get writer's block.

Speed (1994)

Directed by Jan de Bont.

Starring Keanu Reeves, Sandra Bullock, Dennis Hopper.

THE SHORT STORY ★ Dennis Hopper plays a criminal mastermind who rigs a moving city bus to explode if it dips under 50 miles an hour. Reeves plays a young SWAT team cop in for the ride of his life. This thriller features well-rounded characters despite the scorching pace. Things move so fast they should issue a learner's permit with your movie ticket. The 1997 sequel—which Reeves turned down—pales by comparison.

MEMORABLE MOMENT ★ Sandra Bullock as the ultimate nervous driver.

MESSAGE ★ Suddenly walking doesn't seem so inconvenient.

Star Trek IV: The Voyage Home (1986)

Directed by Leonard Nimoy.

Starring William Shatner, Leonard Nimoy, DeForest Kelley.

THE SHORT STORY ★ Serious Trekkies can scoff all they like. This is my personal favorite of the big-screen efforts. The crew of the *Enterprise* boldly go to a time and place where none of them have gone before. Kirk and company time-travel back to the earth of the '80s on the ultimate rescue mission. The humor quotient is a lot higher than usual. But after all these years, it's great to see everyone loosening up for a nice long stretch of laughs.

MEMORABLE MOMENT ★ William Shatner's Kirk trying to explain the unusual behavior of Leonard Nimoy's pointy-eared Spock with an excuse he *thinks* makes perfect sense.

MESSAGE ★ Time-travel at your own risk.

CHECK THIS OUT ★ Want to get serious? Try 1984's *Star Trek III: The Search for Spock*.

Superman (1978)

Directed by Richard Donner.

Starring Christopher Reeve, Margot Kidder.

THE SHORT STORY ★ Richard Donner's big-screen adaptation of the most famous guy ever to don a cape triggered a slew of super-hero films. But this big, bright, speeding bullet of a movie hits the comic book target like no other. There's an affectionate chemistry between Christopher Reeve's Superman and Margot Kidder's Lois Lane that really shines through. The sequels gradually lose steam but this one has enough energy to sweep you along with ease.

MEMORABLE MOMENT ★ Flying with Lois.

MESSAGE ★ It's hard to resist a guy who can leap tall buildings in a single bound.

Time Bandits (1981)

Directed by Terry Gilliam.

Starring Sean Connery, Shelley Duvall, David Warner.

THE SHORT STORY ★ It helps to think of this time-travel fantasy as the smarter British cousin of *Bill and Ted's Excellent Adventure*. It can get just as silly but at least the accents are more sophisticated. Watch for *Monty Python*'s John Cleese as Robin Hood.

MEMORABLE LINE ★ When one character remarks that they've encountered some sort of invisible barrier, another replies, "Oh, so that's what an invisible barrier looks like."

MESSAGE ★ Don't take history too seriously.

CHECK THIS OUT ★ Care for a different spin on time travel? Check out David Warner in 1979's *Time After Time*.

Titanic (1997)

Directed by James Cameron.

Starring Leonardo DiCaprio, Kate Winslet, Billy Zane.

THE SHORT STORY ★ This one virtually defines the meaning of blockbuster. *Titanic* has it all. If you haven't seen this story of a doomed romance aboard the famously ill-fated ocean liner, you're probably highly susceptible to the slightest suggestion of sea sickness. For the rest of us, this may serve as a polite reminder to see it again. It stands up well to repeat viewings and you'll notice something new every time.

MEMORABLE LINE ★ "I'm the king of the world!"

MESSAGE ★ It's better to have loved and lost than never to have loved at all.

Walkabout (1971)

Directed by Nicolas Roeg.

Starring Jenny Agutter, Lucien John, David Gulpilil.

THE SHORT STORY ★ Another cult favorite. Lost in the Australian outback, a teenaged girl and a young boy from the city must rely on an Aborigine youth to help them survive. Not your usual commercial fare. A haunting score and stunning photography take full advantage of the location shoot.

MEMORABLE MOMENT ★ The swimming scene.

MESSAGE ★ Open your heart to different ways of life.

Have You Seen These Classics?

★ ★ ★ ★ ★

The Adventures of Robin Hood (1938)

Directed by Michael Curtiz, William Keighley.

Starring Errol Flynn, Olivia de Havilland, Basil Rathbone.

THE SHORT STORY ★ Remarkably fresh despite its age, this is still the definitive swashbuckler. Errol Flynn was at his peak as the dashing Robin Hood, a princely thief who stole from the rich and gave to the poor. The movie has everything you'd ever want from a classic tale of adventure: great dueling sequences, a stirring score, and playful humor. Wonderful color cinematography is a real plus. There have been many imitators, but they can't top this one.

MEMORABLE MOMENT ★ When Robin Hood meets Little John.

MESSAGE ★ Stealing from the rich should always be this much fun.

The African Queen (1951)

Directed by John Huston.

Starring Humphrey Bogart, Katharine Hepburn, Robert Morley.

Based on the novel by C.S. Forester.

THE SHORT STORY ★ Set in World War I. Take a trip down a dangerously temperamental African river with Rosie and Charlie, two of cinema's most unforgettable characters. As Rosie, Katharine Hepburn is prim and proper. Charlie is a bachelor who likes his gin. Together, these two unlikely traveling companions take on everything from treacherous rapids to the German navy. Bogart won an Oscar for his unforgettable portrayal of Charlie Allnut.

MEMORABLE MOMENT ★ The leeches scene.

MESSAGE ★ You can do anything with teamwork.

E.T. The Extra-Terrestrial (1982)

Directed by Steven Spielberg.

Starring Dee Wallace-Stone, Henry Thomas, Drew Barrymore.

THE SHORT STORY ★ Suburban kids discover a visitor from another planet and try to keep him a secret from the adult world. The best movie of its kind by far. If you can't relate to this one, you should check to see if your heart's still beating. Was Drew Barrymore really once this little?

MEMORABLE LINE ★ "E.T. phone home."

MESSAGE ★ Anything is possible.

Gone with the Wind (1939)

Directed by Victor Fleming.

Starring Clark Gable, Vivien Leigh, Leslie Howard.

Based on the novel by Margaret Mitchell.

THE SHORT STORY ★ In this epic civil war romance, the dashing Rhett Butler meets the impetuous Scarlett O'Hara, and the rest is history. A sweeping saga of love and war in the Old South that's stood the test of time. Some people consider this the greatest movie ever made. Some people just may be right. The multiple Oscar-winner clocks in at nearly four hours. And it's worth every minute of your time.

MEMORABLE LINE ★ "Frankly, my dear, I don't give a damn."

MESSAGE ★ Appreciate what you have while you still have it.

The Great Escape (1963)

Directed by John Sturges.

Starring James Garner, Steve McQueen, James Coburn.

THE SHORT STORY ★ A group of determined POWs plot to escape from a specially designed German prison camp during World War II. There are plenty of great characters here but my personal favorite is Steve McQueen as the "Cooler King." Warning: The movie's catchy theme will play in your head for days. Filmed on location in Germany.

MEMORABLE MOMENT ★ The "pin" scene.

MESSAGE ★ Freedom is worth any price.

CHECK THIS OUT ★ For another take on POWs, try Billy Wilder's 1953 movie *Stalag 17*.

Raiders of the Lost Ark (1981)

Directed by Steven Spielberg.

Starring Harrison Ford, Karen Allen, John Rhys-Davies.

THE SHORT STORY ★ Check your boredom at the door: you won't need it. This period actioneer has so much energy it's like watching an old-time adventure serial on fast forward. Trust me. There's enough excitement in here to satisfy even the most demanding thrill junkie. Harrison Ford stars as archaeologist Indiana Jones. But he doesn't get to spend much time in the classroom. He's too busy trying to save the world. Lucky for us. The two sequels—*Indiana Jones and the Temple of Doom* (1984) and *Indiana Jones and the Last Crusade* (1989)—are both worthwhile. More, please.

MEMORABLE MOMENT ★ Let's just say it involves snakes.

MESSAGE ★ Adventure rules!

CHECK THIS OUT ★ For more exotic adventure, try 1999's *The Mummy*.

Roman Holiday (1953)

Directed by William Wyler.

Starring Audrey Hepburn, Gregory Peck, Eddie Albert.

THE SHORT STORY ★ Audrey Hepburn makes her film debut as a princess who escapes her restrictive lifestyle and is shown another side of life by an obliging reporter. Styles may change but this romance has lost none of its magic over the years.

MEMORABLE MOMENT ★ The gargoyle scene.

MESSAGE ★ Everyone needs a holiday. Even royalty.

> ## Illustrating a point
> Films based on comic books include *Men in Black*, the *Batman* series, *X-Men*, *Josie and the Pussycats*, and *The Phantom*.

Shane (1953)

Directed by George Stevens.

Starring Alan Ladd, Jean Arthur, Jack Palance.

THE SHORT STORY ★ A Western with heart. Alan Ladd plays a mysterious stranger who rides into town and comes to the defense of local homesteaders against greedy cattlemen. Ladd is superb as an ex-gunfighter who can't bring himself to sit back while decent people suffer. Watch out for Jack Palance as one of the most coolly evil bad guys ever to hit the screen.

MEMORABLE MOMENT ★ The final scene.

MESSAGE ★ You *can* make up for your past.

Star Wars (1977)

Directed by George Lucas.

Starring Mark Hamill, Harrison Ford, Carrie Fisher.

THE SHORT STORY ★ George Lucas's masterpiece kicks off what may just be the most popular series in the history of the movies. At heart, this is a Western in outer space. But, like many great films, it combines any number of genres to thrilling effect. A perfect cast gets into the spirit of things to create a film that made Hollywood history with a new generation of stars. This one was created with you in mind. The sequels vary in all sorts of ways but you won't hear fans complaining much.

MEMORABLE LINE ★ "May the Force be with you."

MESSAGE ★ Follow your destiny.

Lasting legacy

Before his death, **Clark Gable** said: "The only thing that kept me a big star has been revivals of *Gone With the Wind*. Every time that picture is re-released, a whole new crop of young moviegoers gets interested in me."

2001: A Space Odyssey (1968)

Directed by Stanley Kubrick.

Starring Keir Dullea, Gary Lockwood.

THE SHORT STORY ★ A complex tale of space exploration that combines elements of drama, horror, and science fiction in an unforgettable mix. You'll never forget HAL 9000, the computer to end all computers. To say anything more would spoil the effect of this masterpiece. Be prepared for a unique ride into unknown territory.

MEMORABLE MOMENT ★ Talking-computer HAL 9000 singing a song.

MESSAGE ★ Be careful out there.

Think About It

★ ★ ★ ★ ★

A thought-provoking movie can have a profound affect on how you come to view a subject. The films in this category cover an enormous range of issues, from the dark satire of *Heathers* to the poignant drama of *My Left Foot*. They can be funny, sad, or romantic. The quality they share is their ability to leave you thinking about them—and your own place in the world — long after the closing scene.

All Over Me (1997)

Directed by Alex Sichel.

Starring Alison Folland, Tara Subkoff, Leisha Hailey.

THE SHORT STORY ★ Set in New York's aptly named Hell's Kitchen, this thought-provoking drama centers around the effect that a tragic gay-bashing incident has on two female friends. The entire cast is great but Alison Folland is particularly memorable as a young lesbian struggling to cope with the gritty realities of life. The punk score is a real plus.

MEMORABLE LINE ★ "So you guys are like sisters?"

MESSAGE ★ Being yourself isn't always easy.

CHECK THIS OUT ★ For a gay-themed film with a whole other take on music, catch 1999's *Trick*.

Almost Famous (2000)

Directed by Cameron Crowe.

Starring Patrick Fugit, Billy Crudup, Kate Hudson.

THE SHORT STORY ★ An affectionate tribute to the power of rock 'n' roll. Patrick Fugit plays a naïve 15-year-old growing up in the '70s. As William Miller, he achieves his dream of becoming a rock writer for *Rolling Stone*. But is William ready to tour with his favorite band? Based on the real life of director Cameron Crowe—who started his career as a rock journalist—this is a coming-of-age movie that blends elements of drama, comedy, and music with admirable skill.

MEMORABLE MOMENT ★ When William tries to sound older over the phone.

MESSAGE ★ Living your dream can be harder than you thought.

Bad Boys (1983)

Directed by Rick Rosenthal.

Starring Sean Penn, Reni Santoni, Esai Morales.

THE SHORT STORY ★ A fascinating look at life in a juvenile prison that pulls no punches. If this one doesn't scare you straight, nothing will. This isn't your typical good guy-bad guy morality tale. It's mostly about the harsh reality of what it takes to survive in a corrupt prison environment. Penn is riveting as a street-smart kid who's prepared to do whatever is necessary to thrive behind bars.

MEMORABLE MOMENT ★ The novel way Penn's character arms himself for an impending fight.

MESSAGE ★ Don't go there.

Bang the Drum Slowly (1973)

Directed by John D. Hancock.

Starring Robert De Niro, Michael Moriarity, Vincent Gardenia.

Based on the novel by Mark Harris.

THE SHORT STORY ★ Moriarity stars as a superstar major-league pitcher who befriends his misfit teammate, a slow-thinking catcher—played brilliantly by De Niro—who's trying to keep his terminal illness a secret from the rest of the team. Have you ever been made a social outcast because of the way you look or talk? This movie puts it all in perspective. It's about a lot of important things. But mostly it's about pulling together in the true spirit of friendship.

MEMORABLE MOMENT ★ The team coach (Gardenia) tries to inspire his bickering players with a speech about squashing a fly.

MESSAGE ★ Even though some friendships can be tough going, they're worth it in the end.

CHECK THIS OUT ★ If you like this one, try 1971's *Brian's Song*. A touching story of friendship on and off the football field.

Benny & Joon (1993)

Directed by Jeremiah Chechick.

Starring Johnny Depp, Mary Stuart Masterson, Aidan Quinn.

THE SHORT STORY ★ Benny (Quinn) is concerned about his mentally ill sister. He tries to find her someone who'll serve as her friend and companion. He discovers an eccentric young man who believes himself to be the reincarnation of silent film comedian Buster Keaton. Top-flight cast with the added bonus of Johnny Depp re-enacting some classic comic routines from the silent era.

MEMORABLE MOMENT ★ Watch for a good reason not to like raisins.

MESSAGE ★ Imagination can heal.

CHECK THIS OUT ★ Johnny Depp in 1993's *What's Eating Gilbert Grape?*

The Boy Who Could Fly (1986)

Directed by Nick Castle.

Starring Lucy Deakins, Jay Underwood, Bonnie Bedelia.

THE SHORT STORY ★ Daughter Milly (Deakins) has to adjust when her widowed mom tries to make a fresh start by moving to a new neighborhood. Things are tough at first. But they start to turn around when Milly befriends a strange neighbor named Eric (Underwood). Locked away in his own fantasy world, young Eric refuses to talk or communicate. In fact, he spends most of his time perched on his roof pretending to fly. But the more Eric withdraws, the more Milly is determined to unlock his secret world.

MEMORABLE MOMENT ★ The clever way Milly's little brother deals with a pesky neighborhood Doberman.

MESSAGE ★ Sometimes change really is for the best.

Conrack (1974)

Directed by Martin Ritt.

Starring Jon Voight, Paul Winfield, Hume Cronyn.

Based on Pat Conroy's novel, *The Water Is Wide*.

THE SHORT STORY ★ Jon Voight portrays a determined teacher dedicated to communicating the joys of learning to deprived black students living on an island off the coast of South Carolina. This one qualifies as an underrated gem.

MEMORABLE MOMENT ★ The farewell scene.

MESSAGE ★ Knowledge is power.

Vocal talents

Winona Ryder *(Heathers, Little Women)* has narrated an audio version of *Anne Frank: The Diary of a Young Girl*.

Dead Poets Society (1989)

Directed by Peter Weir.

Starring Robin Williams, Robert Sean Leonard, Ethan Hawke.

THE SHORT STORY ★ The setting is a conservative, all-male prep school in 1959. The young men enroled there are resigned to boring classes and regimented instruction. Enter John Keating (Williams), an unconventional English teacher who not only loves literature, but encourages independent thought. His passionate philosophy to "seize the day" inspires his repressed students to re-examine their lives. But Keating's bold attitude stirs up more trouble than anyone expects.

MEMORABLE MOMENT ★ When Keating tells his students to tear out the introductory pages of their self-important poetry textbook.

MESSAGE ★ Make the most of every moment life has to offer.

The Elephant Man (1980)

Directed by David Lynch.

Starring Anthony Hopkins, John Hurt, Anne Bancroft.

THE SHORT STORY ★ Based on the true story of Victorian London's David Merrick, a man whose kind and gentle nature is overshadowed by his grotesque physical deformities. John Hurt is brilliant in the title role. It takes a while to get accustomed to his genuinely shocking appearance but hang in there. It's worth it.

MEMORABLE MOMENT ★ The Elephant Man reciting Shakespeare.

MESSAGE ★ Look beneath the surface.

Erin Brockovich (2000)

Directed by Steven Soderbergh.

Starring Julia Roberts, Albert Finney, Aaron Eckhart.

THE SHORT STORY ★ Based on a true story, this is an inspirational movie for anyone who's ever been down on their luck. A determined single mother with no legal experience becomes obsessed with a case involving poisoned drinking water. By thinking of others, she also manages to turn around her own life. Julia Roberts won an Oscar for her performance.

MEMORABLE MOMENT ★ The water-glass scene.

MESSAGE ★ One person *can* make a difference.

Finding Forrester (2000)

Directed by Gus Van Sant.

Starring Sean Connery, Robert Brown, F. Murray Abraham.

THE SHORT STORY ★ Jamal Wallace is a black, inner-city youth who has a rare gift for both basketball and writing. He befriends William Forrester, a neighbor and famously reclusive novelist (played to cranky perfection by Connery). The older man takes Jamal under his wing, encouraging him to make the most of a scholarship to a prestigious prep school. Together, they help each other cope with various fears. Robert Brown makes an impressive debut as the talented and sensitive Jamal.

MEMORABLE MOMENT ★ The intellectual put-down of a mean-spirited professor by Jamal.

MESSAGE ★ We can learn from each other, regardless of age.

Childhood Dreams

As a child, **Julia Roberts** *(Erin Brockovich)* wanted to be a veterinarian. She still loves animals and has hosted a TV documentary entitled: *In the Wild: Horsemen of Mongolia with Julia Roberts*.

The Fisher King (1991)

Directed by Terry Gilliam.

Starring Robin Williams, Jeff Bridges, Amanda Plummer.

THE SHORT STORY ★ A successful radio host begins to question his life after undergoing a personal tragedy. He gets help from an unexpected source—a bright, funny, and emotionally unstable street person played by Robin Williams. A rich and surprising film that makes you think about where your life is heading.

MEMORABLE LINE ★ "There are three things you need in life: respect for all kinds of life, a nice bowel movement on a regular basis, and a blue blazer."

MESSAGE ★ Down and out? It doesn't mean you don't have value.

Forrest Gump (1994)

Directed by Robert Zemekis.

Starring Tom Hanks, Sally Field, Gary Sinise.

THE SHORT STORY ★ A mentally-challenged young man tries to make his way in the world with the aid of his devoted mother; not to mention a little help from his friends. Think of this as a fable that contains some genuinely valuable lessons on life. Director Robert Zemekis employs historical film footage and a memorable score to mark the passage of time. As Forrest, Oscar-winner Tom Hanks pulls the whole thing together.

MEMORABLE MOMENT ★ Forrest on the football field.

MESSAGE ★ As Forrest says: "Stupid is as stupid does."

Gandhi (1982)

Directed by Richard Attenborough.

Starring Ben Kingsley, Candace Bergen, Edward Fox.

THE SHORT STORY ★ Few films are worthy of being called an epic. This is one of them. Ben Kingsley stars in the title role as India's legendary pacifist and statesman. Much more than a history lesson, this sweeping biography is an education in human understanding. It may not make you a better person, but it will definitely show you the path to becoming one.

MEMORABLE LINE ★ Gandhi's philosophy: "My life is my message."

MESSAGE ★ Give peace a chance.

Girl, Interrupted (1999)

Directed by James Mangold.

Starring Winona Ryder, Angelina Jolie, Clea Duvall.

THE SHORT STORY ★ Set in 1967 and based on a true story. Winona Ryder stars as Susanna Kaysen, a self-indulgent young woman who makes a half-hearted attempt at suicide. After being diagnosed with a borderline personality disorder, she's committed to a psychiatric hospital. At first, Susanna uses the opportunity to escape from the outside world. But her experiences with a fellow patient force her to make some hard choices about facing reality.

MEMORABLE LINE ★ "Have you ever confused a dream with life?"

MESSAGE ★ You can try to avoid it but eventually you will have to grow up.

Glory (1989)

Directed by Edward Zwick.

Starring Matthew Broderick, Denzel Washington, Morgan Freeman.

THE SHORT STORY ★ The absorbing story of the first unit of black soldiers to fight on the Union side during the American civil war. An anti-war message, combined with uniformly strong performances, makes this a thought-provoking drama on several levels. Based in part on the letters of the soldiers themselves. Watch for Matthew Broderick in a change-of-pace-role as an inexperienced officer trying to cope with being a leader.

MEMORABLE LINE ★ African-American soldier Denzel Washington explains to his colleagues what he's done since escaping slavery with the quip: "I ran for president … I didn't win, though."

MESSAGE ★ Patriotism can be more complicated than it seems.

Wacky tactics

Robin Williams (*Good Morning, Vietnam, Dead Poet's Society*) won his breakthrough role as an uninhibited alien on the sitcom *Mork and Mindy* with a very unusual audition. Asked to sit down by the show's producer, Williams stood on his head in the chair. During the series, writers left ample space for the comedian to improvise his routines. Called "the Tasmanian devil of comedy" by *Entertainment Weekly*, he is known for his quick wit on the talk show circuit. A couple of typical quips? On drugs: "Cocaine is God's way of telling you you're making too much money." On divorce: "From the Latin word meaning to rip out a man's genitals through his wallet."

Good Will Hunting (1997)

Directed by Gus Van Sant.

Starring Matt Damon, Ben Affleck, Robin Williams.

THE SHORT STORY ★ Working-class guy Will Hunting (Matt Damon) is a mathematical genius who's offered a scholarship to a prestigious university. So what's holding him back? Will has a quick temper and feels emotionally torn by the choice his rare intellectual gift provides. On the one hand, he has a golden opportunity for a new and better life. On the other hand, he has to say good-bye to both his friends and his roots. Which road will he choose?

MEMORABLE MOMENT ★ Middle-aged psychologist Sean McGuire (Williams) has been asked to help the conflicted Will realize his true feelings. Watch for the scene where he attempts to reach his hostile patient by explaining that experience is the true key to maturity.

MESSAGE ★ Doing what's best isn't always easy.

Heathers (1989)

Directed by Michael Lehmann.

Starring Winona Ryder, Christian Slater, Kim Walker.

THE SHORT STORY ★ Tongue-in-cheek satire fueled by the cruel nature of high-school cliques. Veronica (Ryder) hangs around with the three most envied girls in school, all named Heather. The callous way the three Heathers wield their power makes Veronica uncomfortable. But she doesn't do anything about it until she hooks up with the cute but unstable Jason (Slater). Suddenly, the most popular students in school begin to conveniently commit suicide. Dark, edgy humor prevails.

MEMORABLE LINE ★ Jason's take on life can be summed up by what he tells his girlfriend, Veronica. "The extreme always seems to make an impression."

MESSAGE ★ Popularity can be hazardous to your health.

Lean On Me (1989)

Directed by John G. Avildsen.

Starring Morgan Freeman, Beverly Todd, Robert Guillaume.

THE SHORT STORY ★ Tough, no-nonsense principal attempts to turn around a failing inner-city school. Morgan Freeman hits just the right note as "Crazy Joe" Clark, a flamboyant New Jersey educator who uses such unconventional teaching aids as a baseball bat and a bullhorn at close range. Based on a true story.

MEMORABLE LINE ★ Just before an important basic skills test, Clark tells his students: "We sink, we swim, we rise, we fall, we meet our fate together."

MESSAGE ★ Working together toward a common goal is half the battle.

Mask (1985)

Directed by Peter Bogdanovich.

Starring Eric Stoltz, Cher, Sam Elliot.

THE SHORT STORY ★ Eric Stoltz plays Rocky Dennis, a young man whose face has been severely deformed by a rare disease. The movie concentrates on Rocky's relationship with his loving but unconventional mom, a free-spirited biker who teaches her son to make the most out of life. Great performances all around. Rocky's extreme disfigurement may be tough to take at first. But the real joy of this movie is how quickly we see the beautiful person underneath the "mask." Based on a true story.

MEMORABLE MOMENT ✶ A fun house mirror normally distorts your reflection. But when Rocky looks into one, he sees what he was supposed to look like all along.

MESSAGE ✶ As Rocky says: "I look weird, but otherwise I'm real normal."

A step ahead

Men of Honor's **Cuba Gooding Jr.** got an early break in show business by break-dancing at the 1984 Olympic ceremonies. By the time the short-lived dance craze was history, Gooding was on his way to a big-screen career that would ultimately lead to his Oscar for *Jerry Maguire.*

Men of Honor (2000)

Directed by George Tillman Jr.
Starring Cuba Gooding Jr. Robert De Niro, Charlize Theron.

THE SHORT STORY ✶ Based on the true story of Carl Brashear, who overcame extreme prejudice in the '50s to become the first African-American Navy diver. It's fascinating to watch how the grit and determination of Cuba Gooding's Brashear ultimately wins the respect of Robert De Niro's bigoted diving instructor.

MEMORABLE MOMENT ✶ Brashear's final diving test.

MESSAGE ✶ You don't get what you want by quitting.

The Mighty (1998)

Directed by Peter Chelsom.

Starring Elden Henson, Kieren Culkin, Sharon Stone.

THE SHORT STORY ★ Direct opposites Max and Kevin are both being tormented by school bullies. Max (Henson) is big, timid, and scholastically challenged. Kevin (Culkin) is brainy, sarcastic, and walks with crutches. The frail Kevin—known around school as the Freak—could really use a protector. Max has zero confidence and is in desperate need of intelligent advice. The solution? The two loners decide to team up and lend each other support. Together they discover the ability to do great things.

MEMORABLE MOMENT ★ In an effort to evade a gang of pursuing bullies, Max hoists Kevin on his shoulders and wades into a nearby body of water.

MESSAGE ★ The sum of a friendship can be greater than its parts.

My Left Foot (1989)

Directed by Jim Sheridan.

Starring Daniel Day-Lewis, Brenda Fricker, Hugh O'Conor.

THE SHORT STORY ★ Based on the autobiography of Irish writer-artist Christy Brown, who was born with cerebral palsy, this is the inspiring story of a young man determined to beat the odds of a severe physical handicap by simply being himself. The film is always honest, never sappy or manipulative. Oscar-winner Daniel Day-Lewis gives a moving performance. Brenda Fricker, who plays Christy's mother, also won an Oscar. A winner all the way.

MEMORABLE MOMENT ★ When Christy asks a nurse to light his cigarette.

MESSAGE ★ Sometimes your biggest obstacle is the attitude of others.

Norma Rae (1979)

Directed by Martin Ritt.

Starring Sally Field, Ron Liebman, Beau Bridges.

THE SHORT STORY ★ Sally Field won an Oscar for her riveting portrayal of Norma Rae, a textile worker who grudgingly becomes a union organizer. This is a moving portrait of a poor, hardworking and unenlightened woman who gradually realizes that, if she doesn't fight for what she believes in, nobody will. Ron Liebman is memorable as her friend and mentor. Based on a true story.

MEMORABLE MOMENT ★ Norma Rae's attempt to rally the mill workers.

MESSAGE ★ Doing what's right can make you a better person.

O (2001)

Directed by Tim Blake Nelson.

Starring Mekhi Phifer, Josh Hartnett, Julia Stiles.

THE SHORT STORY ★ What if your best friend was not to be trusted, but you didn't know it? This chilling update of Shakespeare's *Othello* moves to a high-school setting, focusing on the basketball team. An uncompromising film that will leave you thinking long after the final scene. Features a young cast sure to have long careers ahead of them.

MEMORABLE MOMENT ★ The "hawk" speech.

MESSAGE ★ Jealousy really is a monster.

CHECK THIS OUT ★ 1995's *Othello* starring Laurence Fishburne.

Ordinary People (1980)

Directed by Robert Redford.

Starring Timothy Hutton, Mary Tyler Moore, Donald Sutherland.

THE SHORT STORY ★ An unflinching look at a remote, dysfunctional family trying to cope with the accidental death of the eldest son. The story turns on the guilty feelings of the troubled younger brother, sensitively portrayed by Timothy Hutton. This won an Oscar for best picture as well as best director and best supporting actor (Hutton). Watch for Mary Tyler Moore as the emotionally damaged mother.

MEMORABLE LINE ★ Hutton as the young son on family life: "The thing that is missing here is a sense of humor. Life is a goddamn serious big deal."

MESSAGE ★ Family matters.

Philadephia (1993)

Directed by Jonathan Demme.

Starring Tom Hanks, Denzel Washington, Mary Steenburgen.

THE SHORT STORY ★ Attorney Andrew Beckett is fired from his conservative law firm because he's a gay man battling AIDS. Not that his cagey superiors will openly tell him his sexuality is a problem, of course. Nevertheless, Beckett decides to sue. The catch? The only person who'll take his case is a small-time, homophobic lawyer who's convinced they don't have a chance. Demme handles the issues surrounding Beckett's dismissal with care and elegance. Hanks's sensitive portrayal won an Oscar.

MEMORABLE MOMENT ★ When Hanks asks lawyer Joe Miller (Washington) to take his case.

MESSAGE ★ Fight for the right to be who you are.

Rain Man (1988)

Directed by Barry Levinson.

Starring Dustin Hoffman, Tom Cruise, Valeria Golino.

THE SHORT STORY ★ Tom Cruise plays Charlie, an irresponsible, self-centered bachelor who discovers that he has an autistic older brother named Raymond (Dustin Hoffman in one of his finest performances). Raymond has inherited the bulk of their father's estate and Charlie is in desperate need of money. Not surprisingly, Cruise decides that he should get to know his highly eccentric brother a little better. The two men get to know each other with surprising results. This one's a must-see.

MEMORABLE MOMENT ★ When Raymond refuses to get on an airplane.

MESSAGE ★ You don't have to be friends with your relatives, but it helps.

CHECK THIS OUT ★ For another complex relationship between two very different brothers, try 1988's *Dominick and Eugene*.

Classical roles

Keanu Reeves *(Speed)* appeared in the lead role in Shakespeare's *Hamlet* on stage in Winnipeg, Manitoba. The role of the Bard's melancholy Danish prince has also proven to be a memorable film role for various actors in recent years. **Mel Gibson** *(Braveheart)* played Hamlet on screen in 1990 while **Kenneth Branagh** *(Much Ado About Nothing)* followed up with his interpretation in 1996. The latest screen version (2000) stars *Dead Poet Society*'s **Ethan Hawke**.

Remember the Titans (2000)

Directed by Boaz Yakin.

Starring Denzel Washington, Will Patton, Donald Faison.

THE SHORT STORY ★ Set in the '70s and based on a true story. Denzel Washington throws himself into the role of a football coach who's hired to ease racial tensions at a Virginia high school. His inspirational approach creates a winning team both on and off the field. The old-fashioned, feel-good approach has all the right moves.

MEMORABLE LINE ★ The new coach's philosophy? "I don't care if you like each other but you *will* respect each other."

MESSAGE ★ United we stand, divided we fall.

River's Edge (1986)

Directed by Tim Hunter.

Starring Crispin Glover, Keanu Reeves, Ione Skye.

THE SHORT STORY ★ A girl you know is murdered and her body left on a riverbank. One of your friends did it. What would you do? This film addresses the question head on and pulls no punches. Dark and deeply disturbing. This one will leave you thinking about your own values. Based on an actual incident.

MEMORABLE MOMENT ★ When Samson (Roebuck) is explaining to Matt (Reeves) why he killed his girlfriend.

MESSAGE ★ It's not always easy to do the right thing.

Romeo & Juliet (1996)

Directed by Baz Luhrmann.

Starring Leonardo DiCaprio, Claire Danes, Brian Dennehy.

THE SHORT STORY ★ The most famous romantic duo in the history of literature get a makeover. Set in contemporary Miami, this has been called Shakespeare for the rock video generation. It's fast, lively, and packed with interesting camera work. But the poetry of it all comes through loud and clear. DiCaprio and Danes have genuine chemistry together.

MEMORABLE MOMENT ★ The first private meeting between Romeo and Juliet.

MESSAGE ★ Parting is such sweet sorrow.

CHECK THIS OUT ★ For the ultimate classic take on *Romeo and Juliet,* Franco Zeffirelli's 1968 version is mandatory viewing.

Scent of a Woman (1992)

Directed by Martin Brest.

Starring Al Pacino, Chris O'Donnell, James Rebhorn.

THE SHORT STORY ★ Chris O'Donnell plays a shy student who accepts a part-time job as the caretaker for a blind man. The man—a retired Army colonel (Pacino) with a healthy appetite for life's pleasures—refuses to sit back and let the world pass him by. He teaches his young caretaker to appreciate the joys of living every day to the fullest. But the brash colonel ends up learning a few things himself.

MEMORABLE MOMENT ★ The tango scene.

MESSAGE ★ Savor each day.

Searching for Bobby Fisher (1993)

Directed by Steven Zallian.

Starring Joe Mantegna, Max Pomeranc, Joan Allen.

THE SHORT STORY ★ A father discovers that his 7-year-old son, Josh, is a chess prodigy. He begins pushing the boy to greater levels of accomplishment until Josh gets tired of the game. Is his dad doing the right thing by forcing his kid to test the limits of his skill? What about the boy's other interests? The plot doesn't sound like much. But you'll be surprised at how absorbing this thoughtful little gem can be.

MEMORABLE MOMENT ★ When Josh first plays chess with his father.

MESSAGE ★ If a game stops being fun, is it still worth playing?

Serpico (1973)

Directed by Sidney Lumet.

Starring Al Pacino, John Randolf, Jack Kehoe.

THE SHORT STORY ★ Based on the true story of Frank Serpico, an honest cop who refused to accept corruption in the New York City police department and paid a high price for his convictions. One of the finest films of the '70s. Tough, thrilling, and unforgettable, but ultimately a tale of morality. Al Pacino's portrayal of the offbeat Serpico made him a star.

MEMORABLE LINE ★ Complaining about Serpico, a crooked officer asks: "Who can trust a cop who won't take money?"

MESSAGE ★ Keeping your integrity is worth any sacrifice.

The Shawshank Redemption (1994)

Directed by Frank Darabont.

Starring Tim Robbins, Morgan Freeman, James Whitmore.

Based on a short story by Stephen King.

THE SHORT STORY ★ An honest man is falsely accused of murder and must learn to cope with life in prison. This is much more than a tale of survival. It's about how you prevail when all hope is lost. As a resourceful inmate struggling to keep alive his faith in the future, Tim Robbins offers just the right mix of patience, grit, and charm. This one's a bit long, but stick around for the ending. You won't be disappointed.

MEMORABLE LINE ★ Tim Robbins's Andy on the irony of his jail sentence. "On the outside, I was an honest man … I had to come to prison to be a crook."

MESSAGE ★ Never give up on the idea of freedom.

CHECK THIS OUT ★ For another story of a man who finds salvation behind bars, try 1962's *Birdman of Alcatraz*.

Smooth Talk (1985)

Directed by Joyce Chopra.

Starring Laura Dern, Treat Williams, Mary Kay Place.

Based on the Joyce Carol Oates short story, "Where Are You Going? Where Have You Been?"

THE SHORT STORY ★ Growing up in the California suburbs, 15-year-old Connie is trying to gain independence while testing her effect on the opposite sex. It's all harmless fun until she begins to flirt with an older man named Arnold Friend (Williams). Arnold seems funny, charming, and sophisticated. But who is he really? A cautionary tale that plays out with admirable subtlety.

MEMORABLE LINE ★ Connie's concerned mother tells her daughter: "I look into your eyes and all I see are trashy dreams."

MESSAGE ★ Be careful who you trust.

Stone Boy (1984)

Directed by Chris Cain.

Starring Robert Duvall, Jason Presson, Glenn Close.

THE SHORT STORY ★ The tragic story of what happens when a farm boy accidentally kills his older brother. An emotionally complex film handled deftly by a superb cast. Heart-wrenching, but well worth the effort.

MEMORABLE LINE ★ "Days are years when it comes to sorrow—there's no such thing as time."

MESSAGE ★ Even when you think you can't go on, you must find a way.

This Boy's Life (1993)

Directed by Michael Caton-Jones.

Starring Robert De Niro, Leonardo DiCaprio, Ellen Barkin.

THE SHORT STORY ★ Set in the '50s and based on the true story of Tobias Wolff's abusive relationship with his stepfather. Robert De Niro delivers one of his finest performances as an alcoholic dad who should never have been a parent in the first place. A harsh, uncompromising look at what happens when a family situation you thought was going to work just doesn't.

MEMORABLE MOMENT ★ Robert De Niro's Dwight coldly informing his new wife of the house rules.

MESSAGE ★ Sometimes your only choice is to leave.

CHECK THIS OUT ★ For another dysfunctional family drama, try 1986's *Desert Bloom*.

A Thousand Clowns (1965)

Directed by Fred Coe.

Starring Jason Robards, Martin Balsam, Barry Gordon.

THE SHORT STORY ★ Barry Gordon plays Nick, a 12-year-old nerd who lives with his free-spirited Uncle Murray (Robards in one of his most memorable performances). Uncle Murray prefers to ignore such stifling social conventions as regular employment. But when a social worker threatens to take Nick away, Murray is forced to take stock of his life. Based on the play by Herb Garner, this is one of my all-time favorites. Do yourself a favor and rent it now.

MEMORABLE LINE ★ Uncle Murray on why he ignores the urgent warnings from utility companies waiting to get paid: "I never answer letters from large organizations."

MESSAGE ★ It's a complicated line between freedom and obligation.

Traffic (2000)

Directed by Steven Soderbergh.

Starring Michael Douglas, Catherine Zeta-Jones, Topher Grace.

THE SHORT STORY ★ This multiple Oscar-winner makes a sincere and brutally honest attempt to get the roots of drug use in our society. It works on many levels, despite juggling a large cast and some complicated issues. Never smug or self-righteous, the movie concentrates on asking important questions. There are no easy answers here. Topher Grace is particularly effective as a privileged, intelligent student who chooses to make drugs a part of her life.

MEMORABLE MOMENT ★ Michael Douglas as a father on a desperate search for a daughter who's lost in more ways than one.

MESSAGE ★ Everything has a price.

Unforgiven (1992)

Directed by Clint Eastwood.

Starring Clint Eastwood, Morgan Freeman, Gene Hackman.

THE SHORT STORY ★ Clint Eastwood stars in this period Western as reformed killer and bounty hunter William Munny. After the death of his wife, Munny comes out of retirement to hunt down a vicious gang of cowboys. He figures he can pull off one last job because he needs the money for his family. But Munny's reputation as a bloodthirsty gunman haunts him wherever he goes. This movie has a lot to say about the difficulty of escaping your past.

MEMORABLE LINE ★ Munny's words to a young man who longs to follow in his violent footsteps. "It's a hell of a thing, killing a man. You take away all he has and all he's gonna have."

MESSAGE ★ Live by the gun, die by the gun.

CHECK THIS OUT ★ For another Western with a similar theme, try John Wayne's *The Shootist* (1976)

Early beginnings

Morgan Freeman (*Glory, The Shawshank Redemption*) spent several years on the popular PBS children's series *The Electric Company* as "Easy Reader." One of his co-stars on the series was **Rita Moreno** (*West Side Story*).

Have You Seen These Classics?

Blackboard Jungle (1955)

Directed by Richard Brooks.

Starring Glenn Ford, Anne Francis, Vic Morrow.

THE SHORT STORY ★ A dedicated educator tries to get through to his students in a school where the tough kids rule over the teachers. This is the movie that started an entire genre. Watch for a young Sidney Poitier in the classroom. One of the first films to feature a rock 'n' roll score.

MEMORABLE MOMENT ★ When the teacher loses his cool.

MESSAGE ★ Some principles are worth fighting for.

CHECK THIS OUT ★ Sidney Poitier moves to the head of the class as a teacher in another classic, 1967's *To Sir with Love*.

Charly (1968)

Directed by Ralph Nelson.

Starring Cliff Robertson, Claire Bloom, Lilia Skala.

Based on the novel *Flowers for Algernon* by Daniel Keyes.

THE SHORT STORY ★ A scientific experiment turns a mentally handicapped man into a genius, but he is emotionally unprepared for the changes in his mental state. Cliff Robertson won an Oscar for his portrayal of a lonely man whose life changes in more ways than one. This drama will really get to you.

MEMORABLE MOMENT ★ Charly's initial intelligence test against a mouse.

MESSAGE ★ Be careful what you wish for.

The Diary of Anne Frank (1959)
Directed by George Stevens.

Starring Millie Perkins, Shelley Winters.

THE SHORT STORY ★ This true story of a sensitive Jewish girl forced to hide from the Nazis has been told on film a few times but this version is still the best. A powerful script combines with a totally committed cast. See it now.

MEMORABLE LINE ★ "In spite of everything, I still believe that people are really good at heart."

MESSAGE ★ We can find moments of joy, even in the midst of seemingly endless sorrow.

Gallipoli (1981)
Directed by Peter Weir.

Starring Mark Lee, Mel Gibson, Bill Kerr.

THE SHORT STORY ★ An Australian masterpiece and unarguably one of the greatest war movies ever made. Set during World War I, this penetrating character study has a youthful, timeless slant. It strips the glory off the idea of combat and makes you take a good long look at the reality of war.

MEMORABLE LINE ★ "War's different. It's just different."

MESSAGE ★ The more things change, the more they remain the same.

M*A*S*H (1970)

Directed by Robert Altman.

Starring Elliott Gould, Donald Sutherland, Robert Duvall.

Based on the novel by Richard Hooker.

THE SHORT STORY ★ Robert Altman's dark comedy on the trials of an army medical unit during the Korean war is a cinematic blueprint for keeping your sanity when everything around you is caving in. First-rate performances combine with the director's unique style to create a work that will last for as long as people get hurt trying to kill each other. This movie also inspired an award-winning TV series.

MEMORABLE LINE ★ "This isn't a hospital. It's an insane asylum."

MESSAGE ★ War is hell but a sense of humor can help you get by.

The Miracle Worker (1962)

Directed by Arthur Penn.

Starring Patty Duke, Anne Bancroft, Victor Jory.

THE SHORT STORY ★ Based on the true story of Helen Keller and the dedicated teacher who helped her to cope with being both blind and deaf. Unvarnished, straight-ahead performances by Patti Duke, as Helen, and Anne Bancroft, as teacher Annie Sullivan, won them both Oscars. Rent the video and count your blessings.

MEMORABLE MOMENT ★ Helen trying to say the word "water."

MESSAGE ★ Every day is a gift.

One Flew Over the Cuckoo's Nest (1975)

Directed by Milos Forman.

Starring Jack Nicholson, Louise Fletcher, Brad Dourif.

Based on the novel by Ken Kesey.

THE SHORT STORY ★ Clever convict Randall P. McMurphy (Nicholson) fakes insanity so that he can serve out his sentence in the relative comfort of a mental asylum. The committed rebel hasn't counted on two things: getting attached to his fellow inmates and engaging in a high-stakes battle of wills with the tough Nurse Ratched (Fletcher). Jack Nicholson gives the performance of his career as McMurphy. But this movie's loaded with great performances all around.

MEMORABLE MOMENT ★ When Nurse Ratched won't allow the inmates to watch the World Series on TV, McMurphy gets back at her by acting out the baseball game.

MESSAGE ★ No matter how hard you try, you can't kill the human spirit.

A Patch of Blue (1965)

Directed by Guy Green.

Starring Sidney Poitier, Elizabeth Hartman, Shelley Winters.

THE SHORT STORY ★ A thought-provoking drama setting in the social and racial backdrop of the '60s. Blinded as a young girl, Selina yearns to break free from her overbearing mother. She is befriended by a kind man and begins to come out of her shell. The catch? She's white and has no idea that the man is black. Sidney Poitier gives a characteristically sensitive performance. Shelley Winters won an Oscar as Selina's bigoted mom but it's

Elizabeth Hartman's Selina you'll remember long after this movie is finished.

MEMORABLE MOMENT ★ Thinking back on the distant days before she was blind, Selina recalls the color of the sky with: "I remember blue."

MESSAGE ★ The things you can't see are more important than the things you can.

CHECK THIS OUT ★ For a lighter take on a similar theme, try 1972's *Butterflies are Free*.

Rebel Without a Cause (1955)

Directed by Nicolas Ray.

Starring James Dean, Natalie Wood, Sal Mineo.

THE SHORT STORY ★ No, the '50s weren't all about Mom's apple pie. In this film, three friends attempt to cope with low self-esteem, dysfunctional parents, and a world that doesn't understand them. Think peer pressure is a new thing? Think again. Despite its age, this film retains a genuine emotional punch. The clothes, hairstyles, and cars are strictly retro. But the message is as contemporary as street racing. If you've only caught James Dean on some faded wall poster, check out this movie and see what all the fuss is about.

MEMORABLE LINE ★ Jim (James Dean) tells his misguided dad: "I want answers now. I'm not interested in what I'll understand 10 years from now."

MESSAGE ★ Growing up can be quite the challenge.

CHECK THIS OUT ★ Interested in more James Dean? Try 1955's *East of Eden*.

To Kill A Mockingbird (1962)

Directed by Robert Mulligan.

Starring Gregory Peck, Mary Badham, Robert Duvall.

Based on the novel by Harper Lee.

THE SHORT STORY ★ A liberal Southern lawyer agrees to defend a poor black man against a rape charge in '30s Alabama. But thanks to the lawyer's two young children, that's only a part of this tender, evocative, and emotionally-charged story. This is simply one of the finest movies ever made. There's a real sense of discovery here, as if you're seeing the truth about life for the very first time.

MEMORABLE MOMENT ★ Lawyer Atticus Finch tells his daughter: "You never know someone until you step inside their skin and walk around a while."

MESSAGE ★ Do what's right, whatever the personal cost.

Fright Night

⭐ ⭐ ⭐ ⭐ ⭐

If you like to be scared, this is the category for you. Some of the best horror films ever made are included here, from Alfred Hitchcock's *Psycho* to William Friedkin's *The Exorcist*. There are also a number of suspense films that should leave you on the edge of your seat. You may think you're up to watching some of these films alone. And maybe you are. But don't say I didn't warn you.

The Abyss (1989)

Directed by James Cameron.

Starring Ed Harris, Mary Elizabeth Mastrantonio, Michael Biehn.

THE SHORT STORY ★ An oil-rig crew embarks on a highly danger-ous mission to rescue a nuclear submarine. Let's just say they have to cope with way more than they bargained for. *Titanic* director James Cameron combines eye-popping special effects with vari-ous twists and turns for a truly thrilling experience.

MEMORABLE MOMENT ★ The scene where two of the crew are about to drown in a damaged submersible.

MESSAGE ★ The ocean is not a nice place.

Aliens (1986)

Directed by James Cameron.

Starring Sigourney Weaver, Carrie Henn, Michael Biehn.

THE SHORT STORY ★ Think of this as the ultimate monster movie in outer space. For my money, this sequel to *Alien* (1979) is far superior to the original. You don't have to see the first one to appreciate the second, but you may find you want to. Sigourney Weaver returns as Officer Ripley, the futuristic space commander intent on getting revenge for the death of her crew at the hands of some of the strangest creatures you'll ever see on the screen. Watch her kick alien butt.

MEMORABLE LINE ★ "We're on the express elevator to Hell."

MESSAGE ★ Outer space is not a nice place.

Alligator (1980)

Directed by Lewis Teague.

Starring Robert Forster, Michael V. Gazzo, Robin Riker.

THE SHORT STORY ★ Your mother told you not to flush that lizard down the toilet, right? Here's what happens when you don't listen. A giant alligator is wreaking havoc on Chicago. The witty John Sayles script mixes comedy with horror for a satisfying blend of laughs and scares. Don't bother with the sequel.

MEMORABLE MOMENT ★ Any time the 2,000-pound alligator gets hungry.

MESSAGE ★ Wouldn't you want revenge if people kept making shoes and purses out of you?

CHECK THIS OUT ★ For more horror with a reptilian spin try 1999's *Lake Placid*.

An American Werewolf in London (1981)

Directed by John Landis.

Starring David Naughton, Jenny Agutter.

THE SHORT STORY ★ A modern twist on the classic tale of how to turn hairy under a full moon. Forget all those corny movies you've seen about the Wolfman. This one has welcome bits of humor but treats the legend with frightening reverence. You *will* be scared.

MEMORABLE MOMENT ★ Watch for the scene with the balloons.

MESSAGE ★ There's nothing romantic about a full moon.

Arachnophobia (1990)

Directed by Frank Marshall.

Starring Jeff Daniels, Harley Jane Kozak, John Goodman.

THE SHORT STORY ★ Do you hate spiders? Then stay away from this film. On second thoughts, if you hate spiders *and* like to be frightened out of your wits, this is the perfect horror movie for you. Lots of humor to balance the extreme creepiness of a giant you-know-what. You'll have a whole new respect for exterminators.

MEMORABLE LINE ★ "They bite?"

MESSAGE ★ Get out the bug spray.

CHECK THIS OUT ★ Up for a vintage horror movie about gigantic mutant ants? Try 1954's *Them!*

The Blair Witch Project (1999)

Directed by Daniel Myrick, Eduardo Sánchez.

Starring Eduardo Sanchez, Heather Donahue.

THE SHORT STORY ★ A film crew is sent to the woods with frightening results. This low-budget effort caused quite a stir when it first came out, prompting numerous TV parodies. Be prepared for lots of shaky camera moves and wool hats. Some people feel this doesn't live up to the hype it got on its initial release thanks to a clever marketing campaign. But it *does* prove that you can scare people on a shoestring budget. Ignore the more expensive but less original sequel.

MEMORABLE LINE ★ "I'm scared to close my eyes. I'm scared to open them."

MESSAGE ★ Don't go into the woods today.

Bram Stoker's Dracula (1992)

Directed by Francis Ford Coppola.

Starring Gary Oldman, Winona Ryder, Anthony Hopkins.

THE SHORT STORY ★ There have been so many movies made about Count Dracula. But thanks to Gary Oldman's performance in the title role, this one gets my vote for the most faithful modern adaptation of the original story. High production values, a great supporting cast, and just the right tone help put this movie over big.

MEMORABLE MOMENT ★ Any scene that features a neck.

MESSAGE ★ If he's looking at your collar for a little too long, be careful.

CHECK THIS OUT ★ For a slight change of pace, try Bela Lugosi in the 1931 classic, *Dracula*.

Buffy the Vampire Slayer (1992)

Directed by Fran Rubel Kuzui.

Starring Kristy Swanson, Donald Sutherland, Paul Reubens.

THE SHORT STORY ★ A high-school cheerleader discovers that she's been specially chosen to kill vampires. The actors look like they're having great fun and Donald Sutherland is particularly memorable as Buffy's tutor in the ways of vampire lore.

MEMORABLE LINE ★ Buffy on moonlighting with her vampire coach: "I can't believe I'm in a graveyard hunting for vampires with a strange man—on a school night."

MESSAGE ★ Girls just wanna kill bloodsuckers.

Carrie (1976)

Directed by Brian De Palma.

Starring Sissy Spacek, Piper Laurie, William Katt.

Based on the novel by Stephen King.

THE SHORT STORY ★ The ultimate horror movie for people who can't stand high-school cliques. Sissy Spacek stars in the title role as an unpopular girl with telekinetic powers. Does she use her gift for the good of humanity? No way. She wants revenge on everyone who's belittled her. Piper Laurie is a whole other kind of scary as Carrie's mom.

MEMORABLE LINE ★ Carrie's religious-fanatic mom tells her, "Pimples are the Lord's way of chastising you."

MESSAGE ★ Putting people down can be hazardous to your health.

Christine (1983)

Directed by John Carpenter.

Starring Keith Gordon, John Stockwell, Alexandra Paul.

Based on the novel by Stephen King.

THE SHORT STORY ★ Can't wait to buy your first set of wheels? This is just the movie to change your mind. Keith Gordon plays a 17-year-old who buys a '58 Plymouth Fury with demonic powers. Like you want the keys *that* bad. A truly different spin on the horror genre.

MEMORABLE LINE ★ "Oh, man, there's nothing finer than being behind the wheel of your own car."

MESSAGE ★ Take the bus.

Cujo (1983)

Directed by Lewis Teague.

Starring Dee Wallace-Stone, Danny Pintauro, Daniel Hugh-Kelly.

Based on the Stephen King bestseller.

THE SHORT STORY ★ If the only celluloid St. Bernard you remember stars in *Beethoven,* you're in for a shock. A mother and her young son are terrorized by a rabid St. Bernard named Cujo. One of the fascinating things about this movie is watching Cujo transform from a playful family pet to a genuinely frightening animal.

MEMORABLE MOMENT ★ Any time the big dog snarls.

MESSAGE ★ Have you ever thought about getting a nice budgie?

Not so scary

The Exorcist's **Linda Blair** starred in a comic spoof of the horror film, 1990's *Repossessed*. Other spoofs of frightening movies include the *Silence of the Lambs* parody *Silence of the Hams* and the *Scream* spoof *Scary Movie*.

Dead Calm (1989)

Directed by Phillip Noyce.

Starring Sam Neill, Nicole Kidman, Billy Zane.

THE SHORT STORY ★ Talk about nowhere to run. A married couple is terrorized by a stranger they pick up at sea. It's marred by gore toward the end, but otherwise this is a superior thriller that relies on intelligence to build tension. Billy Zane is even creepier here than he is in *Titanic*. I guess he just doesn't like boats.

MEMORABLE MOMENT ★ When Billy Zane's Hughie takes over the couple's yacht.

MESSAGE ★ Next time, rent a car.

F/X (1986)

Directed by Robert Mandel.

Starring Bryan Brown, Brian Dennehy, Diane Venora.

THE SHORT STORY ★ Bryan Brown plays a movie special-effects expert who stages the fake killing of a Mafia hit man on behalf of the US Justice Department's Witness Relocation Program. The stunt has more complications than expected, and our hero suddenly finds himself up to his neck in real danger. Fast-paced with—not surprisingly—great special effects. The sequel is almost as good. This also became a TV series.

MEMORABLE MOMENT ★ Any time something blows up real good.

MESSAGE ★ You don't have to know special effects to keep from getting killed, but it helps.

Flatliners (1990)

Directed by Joel Schumacher.

Starring Julia Roberts, Kiefer Sutherland, Kevin Bacon.

THE SHORT STORY ★ I can barely tell one end of a stethoscope from the other, but the medical students in this movie are way smarter than me. As if cramming for exams isn't enough, they decide to conduct experiments with life after death. They kill each other and are brought back to life. All in the interest of science, of course. But what happens when they decide to push the envelope? A little over-the-top at times. Fortunately, a strong cast more than makes up for it.

MEMORABLE LINE ★ "See you soon."

MESSAGE ★ If you work it right, one life is enough.

The Fly (1986)

Directed by David Cronenberg.

Starring Jeff Goldblum, Geena Davis, John Getz.

THE SHORT STORY ★ A no-holds-barred remake of the 1958 cult classic about a scientist who mutates into a human fly. This doesn't have the cheesy charm of the original but Jeff Goldblum throws himself into the role as if he's buzzing around an open bowl of sugar. Prepare for some very intense special effects. Not for the faint of heart. Were you expecting something you could squash with a plastic swatter?

MEMORABLE LINE ★ "Be afraid. Be very afraid."

MESSAGE ★ Is science *really* worth changing life forms?

Fright Night (1985)

Directed by Tom Holland.

Starring Chris Sarandon, William Ragsdale, Roddy McDowall.

THE SHORT STORY ★ A young man enlists the help of an actor turned TV horror-movie show host to slay a vampire that's moved in next door. This one's an obscure gem. Roddy McDowall gives a wonderful performance as a man with a taste for classic horror movies. Avoid the sequel.

MEMORABLE LINE ★ "The kids today don't have the patience for vampires. They want to see some weird slasher running around and chopping off heads."

MESSAGE ★ Do you know your neighbors as well as you think you do?

CHECK THIS OUT ★ In the mood for some vintage horror? Try the great Vincent Price in 1968's *The Conqueror Worm*.

Jaws (1975)

Directed by Steven Spielberg.

Starring Roy Scheider, Robert Shaw, Richard Dreyfuss.

THE SHORT STORY ★ A New England beach town is terrorized by vicious shark attacks. Three guys stand between the shark and his next human buffet: Brody, the town's chief of police (Scheider), Hooper, a marine biologist (Dreyfuss), and Quint, a veteran shark hunter (Shaw). The phenomenal box-office success of this blockbuster launched director Speilberg's famed career and spawned three inferior sequels. Accept no substitutes. This is clearly the best of the four.

MEMORABLE LINE ★ Quint describing the approach of a killer shark: "You know the thing about a shark, he's got lifeless eyes, black eyes, like a doll's eyes. When he comes at you, he doesn't seem to be living … until he bites."

MESSAGE ★ Do you really want to swim *that* much?

Joy Ride (2001)

Directed by John Dahl.

Starring Paul Walker, Leelee Sobieski, Steve Zahn.

THE SHORT STORY ★ Two brothers and a young woman they both want to put the moves on embark on a road trip. Unfortunately, they can't shake off a psycho trucker whom the brothers have alienated along the way. Steve Zahn is perfect as the older brother who keeps whipping himself up into greater levels of panic.

MEMORABLE MOMENT ★ Steve Zahn's Fuller trying to hot-wire a truck while the owner of the vehicle approaches.

MESSAGE ★ Pull over!

CHECK THIS OUT ★ For the original tale of a trucker who loses it, try Steven Spielberg's 1971 cult classic, *Duel*.

Stick with what you know

Director **Alfred Hitchcock** *(Psycho, Rear Window)* once defined drama as "life with the dull bits cut out." He had his own taste of drama as a child when his father had a local police officer slap him in jail to teach him a lesson. A master of suspense, he rarely strayed outside the genre. Even one of his rare comedies—1955's *The Trouble with Harry*— involved a dead body that wouldn't stay put. He once said: "If I make a film of *Cinderella*, people will immediately start looking for the corpse."

Jurassic Park (1993)

Directed by Steven Spielberg.
Starring Sam Neill, Richard Attenborough, Laura Dern.
Based on the novel by Michael Chrichton.

THE SHORT STORY ★ Dinosaurs come back to earth and turn a lot of very nice researchers into used chewing gum. Tacky? Not in the masterful hands of Steven Spielberg. Maybe his secret is that he makes you really care about the people being squished. The dinosaurs on *The Flintstones* never looked like this. Yes, there are sequels but the original is still my favorite.

MEMORABLE MOMENT ★ The first time a dinosaur gets the munchies.

MESSAGE ★ Let sleeping reptiles lie.

The Lost Boys (1987)

Directed by Joel Schumacher.

Starring Corey Haim, Corey Feldman, Kiefer Sutherland.

THE SHORT STORY ★ A unique cross between *Peter Pan* and a high-end gothic vampire movie. A new kid in a California town meets the local gang of troublemakers. What do they do for fun? Suck blood, of course. An interesting twist on the traditional vampire legend. It's a great way to waste time, if you don't take it too seriously.

MEMORABLE LINE ★ A senior citizen's grumpy take on coping with his town's most unusual citizens: "One thing about living in Santa Clara I never could stomach was all the damn vampires."

MESSAGE ★ Vampires come in all age ranges.

Men in Black (1997)

Directed by Barry Sonnenfeld.

Starring Will Smith, Tommy Lee Jones, Linda Fiorentino.

THE SHORT STORY ★ A genuinely funny send-up of the classic alien invasion film that manages to pack in plenty of thrills. A New York cop (Smith) joins forces with a special agent (Jones) to battle an astounding variety of space creatures. At stake? The future of our planet. Moves at breakneck speed. Will Smith is hilarious.

MEMORABLE LINE ★ "Raise your hands and all your flippers."

MESSAGE ★ Just because you're battling aliens doesn't mean you can't have a sense of humor.

CHECK THIS OUT ★ Want to see Will Smith in another tale of alien invasion? Try 1996's *Independence Day*.

Misery (1990)

Directed by Rob Reiner.

Starring James Caan, Kathy Bates.

Based on the novel by Stephen King.

THE SHORT STORY ★ A deranged fan has her favorite writer all to herself after he's seriously injured in a car crash. She nurses him back to health, but she wants plenty in return. Kathy Bates won an Oscar for her portrayal of a psychotic woman who'll do anything to create the plot rattling around in her head. It's the performance of her career. Quite possibly the scariest Stephen King screen adaptation.

MEMORABLE MOMENT ★ When Bates's character tells her writer-captive, "Think of me as your inspiration."

MESSAGE ★ Forget inspiration. Call the cops.

The Omen (1976)

Directed by Richard Donner.

Starring Gregory Peck, Lee Remick, Harvey Stephens.

THE SHORT STORY ★ You think your parents have problems? What would you do if your kid turned out to be son of Satan? This film is genuinely frightening. The parents are played by seasoned pros Gregory Peck and Lee Remick, who give the story a dignity that many horror films lack. The original spawned no less than three sequels. Venture past this one at your own risk.

MEMORABLE LINE ★ Gregory Peck's "Damien!"

MESSAGE ★ Couldn't we just get a pet?

The Others (2001)

Written and directed by Alejandro Amenábar.

Starring Nicole Kidman, Fionnula Flanagan.

THE SHORT STORY ★ Old-style thriller about a young mother who moves into a mysterious mansion with her two children. Sound familiar? Just wait. This plot plays with a conventional ghost story by adding novel twists. For example, the children have a disease that requires them to avoid direct sunlight. This movie proves once and for all that you don't need gore to promote goosebumps. Kidman is exceptional.

MEMORABLE LINE ★ "Sometimes the world of the dead gets mixed up with the world of the living."

MESSAGE ★ Get the moving van.

A Perfect Murder (1998)

Directed by Andrew Davis.

Starring Michael Douglas, Gwyneth Paltrow, Viggo Mortensen.

THE SHORT STORY ★ A stylish update of Alfred Hitchcock's *Dial M for Murder*. A greedy, jealous husband plots to do away with his rich, unfaithful wife. Needless to say, he's a heartless guy. But his plan is so clever you almost want him to get away with it. The intricate plot works just as well as it did for Hitchcock in the '50s. And although Gwyneth Paltrow is no match for Hitchcock's Grace Kelly, she does a great job.

MEMORABLE LINE ★ The nightmare is far from over as Steven (Douglas) tells his distraught wife Emily (Paltrow), "When you wake up tomorrow, all this will seem like a bad dream."

MESSAGE ★ Getting away with murder could be easier than you think.

Planet of the Apes (1968)

Directed by Franklin J. Schaffner.

Starring Charlton Heston, Roddy McDowall, Kim Hunter.

THE SHORT STORY ★ Monkeys rule! At least on a futuristic planet that sees highly intelligent apes turning stranded astronauts into slaves. This is a sci-fi cult classic that actually benefits from some over-ripe acting on the part of Charlton Heston. Let's face it, how can you battle apes and *not* overact? Tim Burton's 2001 remake is slick and competent but a certain sweaty urgency is missing. Give me Chuck any day.

MEMORABLE LINE ★ "Take your stinking paws off me, you damn dirty ape!"

MESSAGE ★ The apes are really out there.

CHECK THIS OUT ★ Catch Charlton Heston in 1973's sci-fi thriller, *Soylent Green*.

Poltergeist (1982)

Directed by Tobe Hooper.

Starring Craig T. Nelson, JoBeth Williams, Beatrice Straight.

THE SHORT STORY ★ Many consider this the ultimate contemporary ghost story. There are plenty of movies about family homes being invaded by supernatural spirits, but this one has to be at the top of the list. The special effects are spellbinding. As usual, the sequel is a watered-down version of the original.

MEMORABLE LINE ★ "They're he-re."

MESSAGE ★ Get out now.

CHECK THIS OUT ★ Still scared? For a friendlier take on the supernatural try the 1990 romance *Ghost*.

Never work with animals...

Director **Tim Burton**'s first film short was an animated tribute to his hero, actor **Vincent Price**. From there, he made a live-action, half-hour film called *Frankenweenie*. IHe then directed his first feature, *Pee Wee's Big Adventure* in 1984. The box office success of that movie led to a wide variety of other work including *Batman* (1989), *The Nightmare Before Christmas* (1993), and *Mars Attacks!* (1996). Speaking on the subject of his remake of *The Planet of the Apes*, he remarked: "You don't know whether chimps are going to kill you or kiss you. They're very open on some levels and much more evil in a certain way."

Rosemary's Baby (1968)

Directed by Roman Polanski.
Starring Mia Farrow, John Cassavetes.
Based on the novel by Ira Levin.

THE SHORT STORY ★ Mia Farrow plays a young wife who finds herself in an unholy alliance with a coven of Devil worshippers. You'll never guess who the father of her baby is. Well, okay, maybe you will, but it's still scary. This was one of the ground-breaking horror films of the '60s. After years of horror stories being told the same way, Polanski's daring approach seemed fresh. It holds up remarkably well today.

MEMORABLE LINE ★ "What's in this drink?"

MESSAGE ★ Two words: Planned parenthood.

Scream (1996)

Directed by Wes Craven.

Starring Neve Campbell, Skeet Ulrich, Drew Barrymore.

THE SHORT STORY ★ This movie is noteworthy because it puts a fresh spin on the horror movie for a whole new generation of fans. The usual slice-and-dice plot is bolstered by a knowing sense of humor and a likeable cast of characters who actually come across as real people. The two sequels aren't nearly as clever.

MEMORABLE MOMENT ★ Any time a conventional horror cliché is challenged by this knowing group.

MESSAGE ★ Don't answer the phone.

Shadow of a Doubt (1943)

Directed by Alfred Hitchcock.

Starring Joseph Cotten, Teresa Wright, Macdonald Carey.

THE SHORT STORY ★ What would you do if you suspected your beloved uncle of being a twisted serial killer? This vintage thriller by the master of suspense has lost none of its power over the years. Teresa Wright is convincing as a young woman who adores her long-lost Uncle Charley on sight—at least at first. This movie has been remade a couple of times. But none of the updates can match the faultless performance of Joseph Cotten as a man whose surface charm masks a dangerous secret.

MEMORABLE LINE ★ Uncle Charley telling his niece, "The same blood runs through our veins."

MESSAGE ★ Appearances can be deceiving.

The Shining (1980)

Directed by Stanley Kubrick.

Starring Jack Nicholson, Shelley Duval, Danny Lloyd.

Based on the book by Stephen King.

THE SHORT STORY ★ Writer Jack Torrance (Nicholson) takes a job as a caretaker in a remote Colorado hotel, figuring it will be a good place to work on his novel. He takes along his wife and son as well. But the company doesn't do him much good. Soon strange things start to happen, and it's all a little too much for Jack.

MEMORABLE LINE ★ "He-re's Johnny!"

MESSAGE ★ You should try to get out more.

Silence of the Lambs (1991)

Directed by Jonathan Demme.

Starring Anthony Hopkins, Jodie Foster.

THE SHORT STORY ★ Hannibal Lecter is a brilliant serial killer who takes perverse delight in striking up an unconventional relationship with a young FBI agent (Foster). How sick is he? Let's just say his taste in people has nothing to do with meeting over dinner. That's because they *are* the dinner. Thankfully, he's locked away in a place where you can't become the main course. But not for long ... Hopkins serves up his best-known performance with flair. Not for the squeamish.

MEMORABLE LINE ★ Hannibal on being tested: "A census taker once tried to test me. I ate his liver with some fava beans and a nice Chianti."

MESSAGE ★ There are some people you just don't need to know.

CHECK THIS OUT ★ For another movie on the reluctant relationship between a psycho and an FBI agent, try 1993's *In the Line of Fire*.

The Silent Partner (1978)

Directed by Daryl Duke.

Starring Elliot Gould, Susannah York, Christopher Plummer.

THE SHORT STORY ★ A psycho frightens a mild-mannered bank clerk into collaborating with him on a robbery. What happens from there is too good to reveal. Brace yourself for moments of violence. Otherwise, sit back and enjoy one of the best cat-and-mouse thrillers ever made.

MEMORABLE MOMENT ★ The mail slot scene.

MESSAGE ★ Sometimes you can call on reserves you didn't even know you had.

Single White Female (1992)

Directed by Barbet Schroeder.

Starring Bridget Fonda, Jennifer Jason Leigh.

Based on a novel by John Lutz.

THE SHORT STORY ★ See this movie before you think about living with a roommate. It's a cautionary tale about what happens when two people *really* don't get along. Allie (Fonda) is looking for a new roommate after breaking up with her boyfriend. She finds Hedra (Leigh) who ends up being the sort of person you don't want to alienate by leaving the cap off the toothpaste, if you know what I mean.

MEMORABLE MOMENT ★ When Hedra dyes and cuts her hair to look exactly like Allie's.

MESSAGE ★ Just how well do you know your roommate?

The Sixth Sense (1999)

Written and directed by M. Night Shyamalan.

Starring Bruce Willis, Haley Joel Osment, Toni Collette.

THE SHORT STORY ★ The gripping, suspenseful tale of a terrified kid who is having disturbing visions and the psychologist who tries to help him. Haley Joel Osment is terrific as the boy who just wants it all to go away. This movie offers much more than chills. It also has a heart.

MEMORABLE LINE ★ "I see dead people."

MESSAGE ★ There are some things we can't explain.

Physical challenge

Former bodybuilding champion **Arnold Schwartzenegger** *(The Terminator, Twins)* on why he started going to the gym: "I was always interested in proportion and perfection. When I was fifteen, I took off my clothes and looked in the mirror. When I stared at myself naked, I realized that to be perfectly proportioned I would need twenty-inch arms to match the rest of me."

The Terminator (1984)

Directed by James Cameron.

Starring Arnold Schwartzenegger, Linda Hamilton, Michael Biehn.

THE SHORT STORY ★ A time-traveling killer robot known as "The Terminator" (Schwartzenegger) is sent from the future to assassinate an unsuspecting woman (Hamilton). The plot gets complicated with various mix-ups, but who cares? The non-stop action is almost as relentless as—you guessed it—the Terminator himself. The special effects are impressive and Arnie plays the first cyborg who looks really cool in shades. Inspired by the works of sci-fi writer Harlan Ellison.

MEMORABLE LINE ★ "I'll be back."

MESSAGE ★ Don't get in the way.

CHECK THIS OUT ★ Cameron's excellent sequel, *Terminator 2: Judgment Day.*

Tremors (1990)

Directed by Ron Underwood.

Starring Kevin Bacon, Fred Ward.

THE SHORT STORY ★ There's a whole lot of shakin' going on in this offbeat tale of giant flesh-eating worms that can burrow underground. Don't like giant worms? Neither do the unfortunate citizens of Perfection, Nevada. But they confront them anyway. Be sure to catch this engaging blend of humor and horror. Bacon and Ward are hilarious as two unlikely heroes.

MEMORABLE MOMENT ★ When the source of local seismic activity is finally discovered.

MESSAGE ★ Anyone want to catch a really big fish?

Twilight Zone: The Movie (1983)

Directed by John Landis.

Starring John Lithgow, Vic Morrow.

THE SHORT STORY ★ This movie is based on the legendary TV series, which featured some of the best writing in the genre. It spruces up some classic stories and strings them together along with a new segment. As in all anthologies, you'll have your own favorites. But this is well worth watching all the way through. It can't quite match the old show but it comes close.

MEMORABLE MOMENT ★ John Lithgow as the airline passenger who sees something he can't believe.

MESSAGE ★ Get into the zone.

Wait Until Dark (1967)
Directed by Terence Young.

Starring Audrey Hepburn, Alan Arkin, Richard Crenna.

THE SHORT STORY ★ A blind housewife is terrorized by a vicious gang looking for a stash of heroin they believe is hidden in her apartment. Audrey Hepburn is totally convincing as Geraldine, the woman who uses her wits to survive the unthinkable. Alan Arkin has never been creepier.

MEMORABLE MOMENT ★ When we're introduced to Geraldine.

MESSAGE ★ Your life can change in an instant.

X-Files: The Movie (1998)
Directed by Rob Bowman.

Starring David Duchovny, Gillian Anderson, Martin Landau.

THE SHORT STORY ★ Admirers of the popular TV series will enjoy the feature film exploits of Mulder and Scully as they continue their quest to explore unexplained psychic phenomena. A little long for non-fans, but a decent effort all the same.

MEMORABLE LINE ★ "Trust no one …"

MESSAGE ★ They're out there.

Have You Seen These Classics?

A Clockwork Orange (1971)

Directed by Stanley Kubrick.

Starring Malcolm McDowell, Patrick Magee, Michael Bates.

Based on the novel by Anthony Burgess.

THE SHORT STORY ★ The tale of a savage future where a gang of heartless social misfits amuse themselves by brutalizing helpless citizens. This bleak, violent satire is not for everyone. But it's undeniably brilliant in its own way. See it for yourself and judge if we're getting closer to this kind of world or not.

MEMORABLE MOMENT ★ Our "hero" listening to soothing classical music.

MESSAGE ★ Don't let it get this bad.

Double Indemnity (1944)

Directed by Billy Wilder.

Starring Fred MacMurray, Barbara Stanwyck, Edward G. Robinson.

Based on the novel by James M. Cain

THE SHORT STORY ★ A conniving woman plots to murder her husband for his insurance money. But that's not all. She drags the guy who sold the policy into the plot. This is one of the best examples of the film noir genre by a master storyteller. Suspense builds slowly but hang in there. You won't be sorry.

MEMORABLE MOMENT ★ On the observation deck of a train.

MESSAGE ★ Greed can kill you almost as fast as a bullet can.

The Exorcist (1973)

Directed by William Friedkin.

Starring Ellen Burstyn, Linda Blair, Max von Sydow.

Based on the novel by William Peter Blatty.

THE SHORT STORY ★ A sweet girl undergoes a horrifying transformation when she is possessed by the Devil. Her mother's desperate solution? Have a priest perform an exorcism. For my money, this is the greatest horror film ever made. That's because it allows the tension to mount in layers before we see anything gory. Dispense with all sequels and accept no substitutes.

MEMORABLE MOMENT ★ When the bed starts to levitate.

MESSAGE ★ You can conquer evil, but only at a price.

Frankenstein (1931)

Directed by James Whale.

Starring Colin Clive, Mae Clark, Boris Karloff.

THE SHORT STORY ★ It doesn't have all the high-tech bells and whistles of a modern horror film but there's something about Boris Karloff's performance as the legendary monster that gets to the heart of this immortal tale like no other version.

MEMORABLE MOMENT ★ The scene by the water with the little girl.

MESSAGE ★ Just because we can do something doesn't mean we should.

CHECK THIS OUT ★ James Whale also directed 1935's *Bride of Frankenstein*.

The Haunting (1963)

Directed by Robert Wise.

Starring Julie Harris, Claire Bloom, Richard Johnson.

THE SHORT STORY ★ Some consider this the best ghost story ever made. The classic tale of a haunted house is given a novel twist when a group of researchers become part of an experiment in the supernatural. Avoid the leaden sequel, which has massive special effects but none of the original's atmosphere.

MEMORABLE LINE ★ "The dead are not quiet in Hill House."

MESSAGE ★ Nowhere is safe.

The writer as actor

Horror novelist **Stephen King** is indeed the king of screen adaptations. His fiction has been the basis for nearly seventy films and TV mini-series. King enjoys doing bit parts as an actor in the films based on his books. He has appeared in various projects as a pizza delivery man, a minister, and a truck driver.

Invasion of the Body Snatchers (1956)

Directed by Don Siegel.

Starring Kevin McCarthy, Dana Wynter.

THE SHORT STORY ★ Pod people take over the souls of normal human beings in this timeless tale of horror. The 1978 remake doesn't quite capture the original's magic.

MEMORABLE LINE ★ "Let's face it. We have a mystery on our hands!"

CHECK THIS OUT ★ For a similar theme in a high-school setting, check out 1998's *The Faculty*.

The Night of the Hunter (1955)
Directed by Charles Laughton.
Starring Robert Mitchum, Lillian Gish, Shelley Winters.

THE SHORT STORY ★ A psychotic con man poses as a preacher to get his hands on a hidden stash of robbery money. First he must befriend the two kids who know where the money is hidden. This is not your average shocker. Moments of tenderness only make the suspense stand out all the more. As the mysterious Rev. Harry Powell, Robert Mitchum makes today's big-screen psychos look like wimps. Don't watch this one alone.

MEMORABLE MOMENT ★ When we see what's tattooed on the preacher's hands.

MESSAGE ★ The world is a delicate balance between good and evil.

No Way to Treat a Lady (1968)
Directed by Jack Smight.
Starring Rod Steiger, George Segal, Lee Remick.
Based on William Goldman's novel.

THE SHORT STORY ★ What happens when a serial killer gets a little too friendly with the cop investigating the case? This cult classic successfully blends elements of comedy, romance, and suspense. The combination is a little different from that in more conventional thrillers but once you get the hang of it, you'll embrace the difference. Packed with great performances.

MEMORABLE MOMENT ★ The opening scene.

MESSAGE ★ Maintaining a close friendship can be murder.

Psycho (1960)

Directed by Alfred Hitchcock.

Starring Anthony Perkins, Janet Leigh, Martin Balsam.

THE SHORT STORY ✭ Forget all the cheap and sleazy horror films out there. You haven't *really* been scared until you've met Norman Bates (Perkins), a peculiar young man who lives with his mother at a creepy little place called the Bates Motel. Guests check in, but they don't check out. Why? Let's just say that young Norman is the key. Shot in chilling black and white by a master of suspense, this classic film changed the horror genre forever. Ignore the 1998 remake and the three cheesy sequels.

MEMORABLE MOMENT ✭ The infamous "shower scene." As a friend put it after watching: "From now on, it's nothing but baths." Enough said.

MESSAGE ✭ Next time, stay at the Holiday Inn.

Cradle to grave

Fright Night's **Roddy McDowall** started out as a child star in the movies, appearing in such vintage films as *How Green Was My Valley* (1941) and *Lassie Come Home* (1943). The late McDowall worked through his adult life in a variety of roles. His distinguished voice can be heard on the Playstation game, "A Bug's Life."

Rear Window (1954)

Directed by Alfred Hitchcock.

Starring James Stewart, Grace Kelly, Raymond Burr.

THE SHORT STORY ★ James Stewart plays a wheelchair-bound photographer who's bored with sitting around waiting for a cumbersome cast to come off his leg. He starts gazing out the window, spying on his neighbors across the courtyard. In the process, he becomes convinced that his mysterious neighbor has murdered his wife. Unfortunately, he has no concrete evidence, so the police don't believe him. Hitchcock layers on the tension with a master's touch. This one will have you on the edge of your seat.

MEMORABLE MOMENT ★ Gathering evidence.

MESSAGE ★ Don't snoop unless you're prepared to accept the consequences.

Just For Laughs

★ ★ ★ ★ ★

When it comes to comedy, I'm not afraid to embrace the stupid along with the wickedly satirical. Some of the films included in this list make me laugh so hard that I have at times snorted various beverages out through my nose. Others mix in a relevant message while making you smile. There are many different styles of comedy represented here, from outright slapstick to dry wit; and many different kinds of characters, from an angst-ridden Woody Allen to a funny-looking green guy named Shrek. But they all have one thing in common: they make us look at the world in a fresh, unconventional, and funny way.

Ace Ventura: Pet Detective (1994)

Directed by Tom Shadyac.

Starring Jim Carrey, Courtney Cox, Sean Young.

THE SHORT STORY ★ Jim Carrey stars as Ace Ventura, a Miami-based private investigator who specializes in recovering lost pets. His latest assignment is to find the kidnapped mascot of the Miami Dolphins football team. You guessed it: it's a missing dolphin. Why would anybody want to steal a dolphin? See this movie and find out. This ace pic launched Carrey's career.

MEMORABLE LINE ★ "Do *not* go in there. Wooo!"

MESSAGE ★ Pets aren't always a guy's best friend.

CHECK THIS OUT ★ If you just can't get enough of Ace, check out 1995's *Ace Ventura: When Nature Calls*.

The Addams Family (1991)

Directed by Barry Sonnenfeld.

Starring Raoul Julia, Anjelica Huston, Christina Ricci.

THE SHORT STORY ★ Think *your* relatives are weird? Spend some time with this ghoulish bunch and your own family will seem boring by comparison. But these certifiable nut jobs do stick together. When someone claiming to be a long-lost uncle shows up, they welcome him with open arms. Based on the *New Yorker* cartoons by Charles Addams, the characters also formed the basis of two TV series. A fun way to embrace the dark side.

MEMORABLE LINE ★ As Wednesday Addams, Christina Ricci explains to her teacher why she's wearing her regular clothes at a Halloween party. "I'm a homicidal manic. They look like everyone else."

MESSAGE ★ Just because you're seriously strange doesn't mean you're also dysfunctional.

Adventures in Babysitting (1987)

Directed by Chris Columbus.

Starring Elisabeth Shue, Keith Coogan, Anthony Rapp.

THE SHORT STORY ★ When her boyfriend cancels out on a date, 17-year-old Chris Parker decides to make some quick money babysitting. She's everything a good babysitter should be. So why does she end up chasing her lost charges all over the mean streets of Chicago? A fluffy, fast-paced no-brainer, but lots of fun if you're in the mood. Elisabeth Shue is especially appealing as a babysitter determined to do the responsible thing—even if it kills her.

MEMORABLE MOMENT ★ The scene in an after-hours blues club.

MESSAGE ★ How badly do you want to earn a little extra cash?

Airplane! (1980)

Directed by Jim Abrahams, David Zucker, Jerry Zucker.

Starring Robert Hays, Julie Hagerty, Robert Stack.

THE SHORT STORY ★ The mother of all disaster movie parodies, *Airplane!* was so successful it unleashed a flood of imitators. When an entire airline crew becomes ill due to food poisoning, it's up to ex-Navy pilot Ted Striker to save the passengers from a terrible fate. But Striker has developed a phobia about piloting aircraft. The humor here can fly pretty low when it comes to puns and sight gags but thanks to a perfect cast it works great.

MEMORABLE LINE ★ "Don't call me Shirley!"

MESSAGE ★ Next time, take the train.

All of Me (1984)

Directed by Carl Reiner.

Starring Steve Martin, Lily Tomlin, Victoria Tennant.

THE SHORT STORY ★ This movie gives a whole new meaning to the phrase "split personality." Steve Martin plays a young lawyer who's forced to share his body with the soul of a dead woman after a spiritual experiment in soul transference backfires. Lily Tomlin—who is mostly limited to playing a voice inside Martin's head—portrays the cranky woman attempting to gain complete control over her new body. But it's Martin's comic struggle to appear normal that prompts most of the laughs.

Seriously funny

Frantic funnyman **Mel Brooks** (*Blazing Saddles, Young Frankenstein*) has consistently refused to direct dramatic films, explaining "It wouldn't be as much fun as delivering my dish of insanity." Brooks does have a definite serious side, however. He has written romantic ballads and has produced some notable dramatic films through his company Brooksfilms, including *84 Charing Cross Road*, and *The Elephant Man*. Both films featured his wife, *The Miracle Worker*'s **Anne Bancroft**. He once confessed to a reporter that he transformed the Frankenstein story into a comedy as a way of dealing with recurring childhood nightmares. "Maybe part of the reason for doing *Young Frankenstein* was to make it terribly funny so I'd never have those dreams again."

MEMORABLE MOMENT ★ When our lawyer hero begins to develop a feminine gait, he instructs his new soulmate to try walking like a man.

MESSAGE ★ Sometimes it's possible for a couple to be a little *too* close.

CHECK THIS OUT ★ For more mixed-up Martin, try 1983's *The Man with Two Brains*.

American Pie (1999)
Directed by Paul Weitz.
Starring Jason Biggs, Shannon Elizabeth, Chris Klein.

THE SHORT STORY ★ Four teenaged guys vow to lose their virginity before prom night. This slice of hormonally-charged amusement is not for the easily offended. Driven by crude, outrageous humor and a likeable cast of horndogs, it *does* have a few genuinely thoughtful moments. But the most infamous scene—involving the gross abuse of totally innocent pastry—is a shabby attempt to cash in at the box office. For shame. You're still going to watch it, right? The sequel does not involve baked goods.

MEMORABLE LINE ★ On the subject of going off to college with no sexual experience Jim (Biggs) quips: "They probably have special dorms for people like us."

MESSAGE ★ Losing your innocence may not be worth all the hassle.

CHECK THIS OUT ★ If you like Jason Biggs, catch him in Amy Heckerling's *The Loser* (2000).

Austin Powers: International Man of Mystery (1997)

Directed by Jay Roach.

Starring Mike Myers, Elizabeth Hurley, Michael York.

THE SHORT STORY ★ Who is Austin Powers? A groovy secret agent from the '60s who's suddenly defrosted after decades of being cryogenically frozen. His mission is to do battle with the diabolical Dr. Evil. Mike Myers is hilarious in the dual roles of Powers and Dr. Evil. A delicious send-up of the James Bond films. 1999's sequel—*The Spy Who Shagged Me*—is on par with the original.

MEMORABLE LINE ★ Austin's catch phrase: "Yeah, Ba-by!"

MESSAGE ★ Bring back the '60s at your own risk.

Beetle Juice (1988)

Directed by Tim Burton.

Starring Michael Keaton, Alec Baldwin, Geena Davis.

THE SHORT STORY ★ A recently deceased couple (Baldwin and Davis) try to scare away the annoying family that's moving into their beloved home. Unfortunately, they're just too nice to be effective as nasty ghosts. Not to be defeated, they bring in a pasty-faced ghoul known as Betelguese (Keaton at his comic best). Fast-moving with great special effects.

MEMORABLE LINE ★ "I'm the ghost with the most, babe."

MESSAGE ★ When you gotta go, you gotta go.

Bill and Ted's Excellent Adventure (1989)

Directed by Stephen Herek.

Starring Keanu Reeves, Alex Winter, George Carlin.

THE SHORT STORY ✱ Two really dumb guys need a way to pass history class. The solution? A magical telephone booth that allows them to travel back and forth through time with such key historical figures as Napoleon, Joan of Arc, and Abraham Lincoln. An excellent time-waster, though I feel compelled to add a language warning. History may repeat itself, but not nearly as often as these Valley guys use words like dude and radical.

MEMORABLE LINE ✱ Bill (Winter) commenting on the pair's dismal academic performance: "We are about to fail most egregiously."

MESSAGE ✱ And you thought your best friend could be stupid.

CHECK THIS OUT ✱ Bill and Ted travel through Heaven and Hell in the radical sequel *Bill and Ted's Bogus Journey*.

Singular success

After the British comedy troupe Monty Python split up, all its members went on to individual projects with varying degrees of success. **John Cleese** starred in *A Fish Called Wanda*, among other movies, and made guest appearances in such sitcoms as *Cheers* and *Third Rock From the Sun*. **Eric Idle** appeared in *National Lampoon's European Vacation*. **Terry Gilliam** directed *Brazil*, *The Fisher King*, and *The Adventures of Baron Munchausen*. **Michael Palin** has hosted such travel-based adventure specials as *Around the World in 80 Days*.

Blazing Saddles (1974)

Directed by Mel Brooks.

Starring Gene Wilder, Cleavon Little, Madeline Kahn.

THE SHORT STORY ★ Welcome to Rock Ridge, the craziest town in the Old West. If this Western spoof doesn't leave your sides hurting from laughing too hard, you should forget this kind of movie altogether. Brooks turns the conventions of the classic cowboy movie upside down for the sake of laughs. Along the way, he also manages to make a lot of clever points about racial and movie stereotypes. The film moves at such a wild pace that you can barely keep up with the gags.

MEMORABLE MOMENT ★ Watch for the notorious campfire scene.

MESSAGE ★ The Old West can teach us new things.

Bring It On (2000)

Directed by Peyton Reed.

Starring Kirsten Dunst, Eliza Dushku, Jesse Bradford.

THE SHORT STORY ★ Two high-school cheerleading teams take aim at the national championship. The five-time champions from San Diego's Rancho Carne High look like the best bet—until the new team captain discovers that all their award-winning routines were stolen from another school. Will they create an original routine on time? Will their ripped-off rivals get revenge? Like the movie's tagline says: "May the best moves win." Sure, it's over the top. But this one has attitude to spare.

MEMORABLE MOMENT ★ Pick a cheerleading scene. *Any* cheerleading scene.

MESSAGE ★ Pom-poms aren't for wimps.

Clueless (1995)

Directed by Amy Heckerling.

Starring Alicia Silverstone, Stacey Dash, Paul Rudd.

THE SHORT STORY ★ Cher Horowitz is a wealthy and popular Beverly Hills teenager. But, along with her best friend Dione, she soon discovers there's more to life than shopping till you drop. Why keep your incredibly good taste to yourself when you can help someone in desperate need of a makeover? So the two girls befriend a "clueless" exchange student and teach her the ways of California cool. A big-hearted comedy loosely based on Jane Austen's novel *Emma*.

MEMORABLE LINE ★ "As *if*!"

MESSAGE ★ Friendship has a style all its own.

Cool Runnings (1993)

Directed by Jon Turteltaub.

Starring John Candy, Leon, Doug E. Doug.

THE SHORT STORY ★ This film is based on the true story of a Jamaican bobsled team training for the 1988 Winter Olympics. Talk about long shots. Our game competitors have never even seen snow never mind ridden on a bobsled. A feel-good movie that's surprisingly sophisticated for a Disney offering. John Candy gives one of his most effective performances as a former disgraced bobsledder with one last chance to get back on track. Will he redeem himself by coaching his guys to glory?

MEMORABLE MOMENT ★ The bobsled prayer.

MESSAGE ★ Try it. You'll like it—if you don't end up in the hospital first.

Dick (1999)

Directed by Andrew Fleming.

Starring Kirsten Dunst, Michelle Williams, Dan Hedaya.

THE SHORT STORY ★ Political history was never this much fun. Dunst and Williams play two fun-loving best friends who stumble on all the elements leading up to the Watergate scandal. How smart are our heroines? Let's just say one of them thinks Richard Nixon is a hunk. But don't let that put you off. Thanks to Dan Hedaya's hilarious portrayal of Nixon, this is a lot funnier than watching *All the President's Men*.

MEMORABLE MOMENT ★ Watch the girls as they leaf through a scrapbook that makes Nixon seem like he should be on the cover of *Seventeen*.

MESSAGE ★ Don't develop a crush on the president. Even if he says he's not a crook.

Upsizing

The late **John Candy** (*Uncle Buck, Cool Runnings*) was a TV alumni of the Canadian-based sketch comedy *SCTV*. Several other members of the troupe also made the successful transition to movies. They include **Eugene Levy** (*American Pie*), **Catherine O'Hara** (*Beetle Juice*) and **Rick Moranis** (*Spaceballs*).

Dumb and Dumber (1994)

Directed by Peter Farrelly.

Starring Jim Carrey, Jeff Daniels, Lauren Holley.

THE SHORT STORY ★ Turn off your brains for this goof-fest, which works very hard to live down to its title. Jeff Daniels (dumb) and Jim Carrey (dumber) play two of the stupidest slackers you'll ever see onscreen. Both of them are attracted to Mary (Holly), a pretty and intelligent woman who misplaces her suitcase. When our heroes find the suitcase, they decide to return it to her via a road trip to Aspen. If there were an Oscar for bad haircuts, this movie would win hands down. Warning: Toilet humor alert.

MEMORABLE MOMENT ★ What happens if nature calls in a moving car and you don't have time to stop? See this movie and find out.

MESSAGE ★ Your life may be going down the sewer. But if you're too dumb to care, the trip won't be so bad.

It pays to have goals

At the age of 10, **Jim Carrey** sent his resume into the popular comedy/variety hour, *The Carol Burnett Show*. In junior high, he was given a few minutes each day to perform his comedy routines in front of his classmates. There was a catch, however—he had to behave himself for the rest of the day. For years, the struggling comedian kept a check in his wallet, which he had made out to himself for the amount of $20 million. He reportedly stopped carrying the check around the time he actually earned $20 million from *The Cable Guy*.

Ed Wood (1994)

Directed by Tim Burton.

Starring Johnny Depp, Martin Landau, Sarah Jessica Parker.

THE SHORT STORY ★ The quirky story of Ed Wood, easily the world's worst—if most enthusiastic—movie director. This oddball comic biography of the man who gave us such turkeys as *Plan Nine from Outer Space* may take a little getting used to. There's not much plot or action, but take my advice and hang in there. This one has many rewards for the patient viewer. Martin Landau is wonderful as aging horror star Bela Lugosi, who was best known for his vintage portrayal of Dracula.

MEMORABLE MOMENT ★ Watching Landau rise from his coffin, long after he's hung up his vampire cape.

MESSAGE ★ Talent and enthusiasm don't always go hand in hand.

Election (1999)

Directed by Alexander Payne.

Starring Matthew Broderick, Reese Witherspoon, Chris Klein.

THE SHORT STORY ★ Semi-dark satire about a Nebraska high-school teacher who's bothered by the fact that one of his seriously overachieving students is running unopposed for class president. Witherspoon gets top marks as a perky, super-organized know-it-all who pushes all the wrong buttons in her envious teacher. Broderick has great fun playing a guy whose life peaked during his days as a high-school student. Think of it as the flip side to Broderick's role in *Ferris Bueller's Day Off*.

MEMORABLE LINE ★ "Just tell me who won!"

MESSAGE ★ Here's a scary thought. Maybe your high-school years really *are* the best years of your life.

Fast Times at Ridgemount High (1982)

Directed by Amy Heckerling.

Starring Sean Penn, Judge Reinhold, Jennifer Jason Leigh.

THE SHORT STORY ★ The majority of this young cast went on to film stardom that's stretched over the last twenty years. It's not hard to see why. This look at life in a California high school is packed with moments that are as funny as they are true. Sure, it was made in the early '80s but in many ways, this movie is still as fresh as a newly waxed surfboard. Anybody who's ever worked for slave wages in a fast-food place should see this movie immediately.

MEMORABLE MOMENT ★ Sean Penn's Spicoli ordering pizza in class.

MESSAGE ★ Ride the curl while you still can.

Ferris Bueller's Day Off (1986)

Directed by John Hughes.

Starring Matthew Broderick, Alan Ruck, Jeffrey Jones.

THE SHORT STORY ★ Broderick stars as Ferris, the ultimate high-school con artist and class-cutter. Skipping out of school to enjoy a glorious day of total freedom in the big city, the cunning but loveable Ferris convinces his buddies to come along. Soon their high-strung principal (Jones) is in hot pursuit. Will Ferris get busted? Will his principal have a nervous breakdown? See this movie before you even *think* of skipping out.

MEMORABLE MOMENT ★ The way Ferris convinces his best friend to surrender the keys to his dad's prized sports car.

MESSAGE ★ Sometimes a guy just needs a mental health day.

Ghostbusters (1984)

Directed by Ivan Reitman.

Starring Bill Murray, Dan Aykroyd, Harold Ramis.

THE SHORT STORY ★ Three offbeat scientists lose their university positions and decide to investigate the field of paranormal pest control. They start a New York-based business as professional Ghostbusters. Their mission? To exterminate troublesome spirits and ghouls faster than you can say "proton gun." But the guys get in a little over their heads when they discover the gateway to another dimension. The phenomenon threatens to wreak havoc on their beloved city. Will they become ghost toast? Watch this one and find out.

MEMORABLE LINE ★ As someone thrashes about in the midst of demonic possession, Bill Murray's Dr. Venkman quips: "I think we can get her a guest spot on *The Wild Kingdom*."

MESSAGE ★ Impending doom can have a funny side

Groundhog Day (1993)

Directed by Harold Ramis.

Starring Bill Murray, Andie MacDowell, Chris Elliot.

THE SHORT STORY ★ Ever wish you could experience a particular day more than once? That's exactly what happens to Bill Murray as a self-absorbed weatherman who finds himself reliving the same 24 hours over and over. We never find out why this is happening. But the script is so clever it doesn't really matter.

MEMORABLE LINE ★ "What if there *is* no tomorrow? There wasn't one today."

MESSAGE ★ Sometimes you need a second chance. Then another. And then another …

Happy Gilmore (1996)

Directed by Dennis Dugan.

Starring Adam Sandler, Christopher McDonald, Julie Bowen.

THE SHORT STORY ★ Former *Saturday Night Live* comic Sandler stars in the title role as a hapless hockey player turned pro golfer. Happy—who is anything but—brings his brawling, belligerent ways to the tranquil game with some funny results. Wait till you see this guy putt.

MEMORABLE MOMENT ★ Happy duking it out with game-show host Bob Barker.

MESSAGE ★ Golf is tougher than you think.

CHECK THIS OUT ★ For more Sandler, try 1998's *The Waterboy*.

House Party (1990)

Directed by Ellen Brown, Reginald Hudlin.

Starring Christopher Reid, Robin Harris, Christopher Martin.

THE SHORT STORY ★ A rap twist on what happens when a teenager's house party gets out of hand. Hot, young actors give the standard plot a fresh and energetic take. Music a definite plus but it's the film's basic sweetness that will win you over.

MEMORABLE LINE ★ "Hey, you! Eraserhead."

MESSAGE ★ You can't stop the music. Even when you try to turn it down.

CHECK THIS OUT ★ Want to find out what happens to the characters in *House Party*? There are two sequels: *House Party 2* (1991) and *House Party 3* (1994).

Legally Blonde (2001)

Directed by Robert Luketic.

Starring Reese Witherspoon, Luke Wilson, Victor Garber.

THE SHORT STORY ★ At first glance, the life of Elle Woods seems as golden as her hair. She belongs to the right sorority, dates the cutest guy on campus, and obviously uses the right conditioner. But when Elle's Harvard-bound boyfriend dumps her for some-one he considers more cerebral, she follows him into law school. Reese Witherspoon stars as the feisty Elle, giving new meaning to the phrase "blonde ambition."

MEMORABLE MOMENT ★ Fashion merchandising major Elle on color preference: "Whoever said orange was the new pink was seriously disturbed."

MESSAGE ★ You are more than the color of your hair.

Life's lessons

Would you believe that **Reese Witherspoon** was stood up by her date for the high school prom? She ended up going with her dad. On the ups and downs of life, she once told a reporter, "I even feel glad that I've experienced some failure in my life. That gives you perspective and humility about this business."

Meatballs (1979)

Directed by Ivan Reitman.

Starring Bill Murray, Kate Lynch, Chris Makepeace.

THE SHORT STORY ★ Goofy but surprisingly endearing. This comedy about summer camp—which features Murray as an off-the-wall counsellor—isn't as slick as some of Reitman's later work. It has the cheap look of a rundown cabin and some of the "kids" seem a little old for camp. But *Meatballs* makes up for its shortcomings with a lot of heart. Unlike some similar comedies, this movie is actually about something. Beware of the Murray-less sequels.

MEMORABLE MOMENT ★ Murray's nervous campers are about to enter a race with their arch rivals. He loosens them up by getting them to chant, "It just doesn't matter!"

MESSAGE ★ You can accomplish more than you think.

Mouse Hunt (1997)

Directed by Gore Verbinski.

Starring Nathan Lane, Lee Evans, Vicki Lewis.

THE SHORT STORY ★ Two brothers inherit a mansion with a pesky rodent as the sole tenant. Impressive physical comedy ensues as the pair do everything they can to exterminate their unwelcome guest. How much trouble can one rodent cause? Just watch and find out. This movie is a little on the long side but the antics of Lane and Evans are the closest thing you'll find to a modern-day Laurel and Hardy.

MEMORABLE MOMENT ★ When our incompetent pair set a few too many mousetraps.

MESSAGE ★ Pest control can drive you crazy.

CHECK THIS OUT ★ If this whets your appetite for pure slapstick, try anything by The Three Stooges or Laurel and Hardy.

National Lampoon's Christmas Vacation (1989)

Directed by Jeremiah S. Chechik.

Starring Chevy Chase, Beverley D'Angelo, Randy Quaid.

THE SHORT STORY ★ You gotta love the Griswolds, especially around Christmas. Slightly twisted holiday favorite that many fans of this series consider the best of the bunch. Chevy Chase stars as the hapless dad who's just trying to hold his loopy family together over the Yuletide festivities. Slapstick and low humor carry the film, but there are surprising dashes of warmth here.

MEMORABLE MOMENT ★ Setting up the Christmas tree.

MESSAGE ★ Just because your family's bizarre doesn't mean you can't enjoy Christmas.

CHECK THIS OUT ★ The Griswolds are featured in three other comedies. Try the first one, 1983's *National Lampoon's Vacation*.

Funny and smart

Elizabeth Shue (*Adventures in Babysitting*) majored in government at Wellesley College before transferring to Harvard University. She left to pursue an acting career, but returned to complete her degree. **Sigourney Weaver** (*Ghostbusters*) attended Stanford and the Yale School of Drama. Her real name is Susan—she adopted the name Sigourney from a character in F. Scott Fitzgerald's *The Great Gatsby*.

Risky Business (1983)

Directed by Paul Brickman.

Starring Tom Cruise, Rebecca De Mornay, Bronson Pinchot.

THE SHORT STORY ★ A frantically-paced comedy about the disastrous things that can happen when your parents go out of town and decide to trust you with the keys to the house and the sports car. The over-the-top script stretches credibility at times, but this winner ranks as one of the definitive teen comedies of the '80s. Tucked underneath all the fun is a trenchant message about greed and values. This was the breakthrough film for Cruise, who never looked back.

MEMORABLE LINE ★ "Porsche. There *is* no substitute!"

MESSAGE ★ Money isn't everything, except when you really need it.

Romy and Michele's High-School Reunion (1997)

Directed by David Mirkin.

Starring Mira Sorvino, Lisa Kudrow, Janeane Garofalo.

THE SHORT STORY ★ Two flighty young women decide to attend their 10-year high-school reunion. Their mission? To stir up envy in the people who made their high-school years so miserable. They haven't done that well since graduating, but that doesn't stop Romy and Michele. They simply invent the lives they *should* be leading. What could possibly go wrong?

MEMORABLE LINE ★ "Have a Romy and Michele day!"

MESSAGE ★ Two heads are better than one. Sometimes.

Shrek (2001)

Directed by Andrew Adamson, Vicki Jensen, Scott Marshall.

Starring the voices of Mike Myers, Eddie Murphy, Cameron Diaz.

THE SHORT STORY ★ In this animated gem, Shrek is an ogre who keeps to himself in the woods. The guy has his reasons. He's bald, green, and shaped like an overgrown fire hydrant. On the plus side, he has a heart of gold. His sidekick—a mouthy donkey voiced by Eddie Murphy—sees the best in Shrek. The donkey feels that his pal deserves a shot at the beautiful Princess Fiona. The problem? Fiona is set to marry the horizontally challenged Lord Farquad, a pompous twit who'll make the princess miserable.

MEMORABLE MOMENT ★ The musical number "I'm a Believer."

MESSAGE ★ Heroes come in all shapes and sizes.

Sleeper (1973)

Directed by Woody Allen.

Starring Woody Allen, Diane Keaton, John Beck.

THE SHORT STORY ★ Woody Allen stars as the nerdy Miles Monroe. Experimentally frozen in 1973, Miles wakes up 200 years later to discover a world where junk food is good for you and people have stopped thinking for themselves. He reluctantly joins an underground movement to defeat an evil dictator. But there's not much of the dictator left after a bomb attack. Monroe's challenge? Steal the guy's nose to prevent it from being cloned. Plenty of slapstick keeps this one moving.

MEMORABLE LINE ★ Fellow revolutionary Luna (Diane Keaton) is amazed that the hibernating Miles has not had sex in 200 years. Corrects Miles: "Two hundred and four—if you count my marriage."

MESSAGE ★ Sometimes waking up is worth it.

Spaceballs (1987) Directed by Mel Brooks.

Starring John Candy, Rick Moranis, Bill Pullman.

THE SHORT STORY ✳ Actor/director Mel Brooks bends the serious space movie out of shape. See this one after *Star Wars* or it'll ruin both movies for you. Watch for Brooks as the wise "Yogurt."

MEMORABLE MOMENT ✳ The classic Brooks take on Darth Vader.

MESSAGE ✳ May the Force knock you on your butt.

From the small screen

Television comedy series have proved to be a great stepping stone to making movies for a wide variety of performers. *Men in Black*'s **Will Smith** began his acting career in the sitcom *The Fresh Prince of Bel Air*. **Leonardo DiCaprio** got his first break with a regular role on TV's *Growing Pains*; and **Lisa Kudrow** of *Romy and Michele's High School Reunion* is well known from the sitcom *Friends*. **Bill Murray** is just one of many graduates from TV's *Saturday Night Live* to make the successful leap into feature films. Fellow *SNL* alumni who made their mark on the big screen include **John Belushi, Chevy Chase, Mike Myers, Eddie Murphy,** and **Adam Sandler**. Other notable movie personalities who got their start acting in television comedies include such directors as **Ron Howard** (*The Andy Griffith Show)*, **Rob Reiner** (*All in the Family*), and **Penny Marshall** (*Laverne and Shirley*).

Stripes (1981)

Directed by Ivan Reitman.

Starring Bill Murray, Harold Ramis, Warren Oates.

THE SHORT STORY ★ For my money, this is the funniest movie that's ever been made about army life. Bill Murray and Harold Ramis play a pair of unmotivated losers who decide to give their lives some much-needed direction by joining the military. Unfortunately, these guys aren't cut out to follow the rules. Warren Oates gives a memorable performance as the excitable drill sergeant determined to whip them into shape.

MEMORABLE MOMENT ★ As a reluctant soldier, Bill Murray cautions his sergeant against sending the men into the rain for maneuvers. He wisely points out that it's the height of flu season.

MESSAGE ★ Orders are made to be broken.

CHECK THIS OUT ★ Want a female spin on the tribulations of army life? Be sure to catch Goldie Hawn in 1980's *Private Benjamin*.

This Is Spinal Tap (1984)

Directed by Rob Reiner.

Starring Christopher Guest, Michael McKean, Harry Shearer.

THE SHORT STORY ★ A comic parody of a rock documentary featuring the members of Spinal Tap. We watch as the fading Heavy Metal band limps through a disastrous American tour. How bright are these shaggy-haired Englishmen? Let's just say they're a few bulbs shy of an amp. The lads do know *one* thing. If you can't be good, you can at least be loud. The bonus? A few minutes of this, and your own garage band will start to sound a whole lot better.

MEMORABLE MOMENT ★ Band member Nigel Tufnel (Guest) proudly explains that, while most amplifiers only go up to 10, his goes all the way to 11.

MESSAGE ★ If music is your life, sometimes you're better off dead.

Trading Places (1983)

Directed by John Landis.

Starring Dan Aykroyd, Eddie Murphy, Jamie Lee Curtis.

THE SHORT STORY ★ A clever yuppie twist on the classic story of *The Prince and the Pauper*. Two rich old codgers decide to conduct a psychological experiment by drastically altering the lives of two very different people. First, they strip a rich stockbroker of his rights and privileges. Then they give everything to a shifty con man who doesn't have a nickel to his name. What will their experiment yield? Lots of laughs, for a start. This is Eddie Murphy at his very best.

MEMORABLE MOMENT ★ When Dan Aykroyd's penniless stock-broker pounds on the door of his mansion only to have his very own butler turn him away.

MESSAGE ★ Fate can bring out the best in us.

Twins (1988)

Directed by Ivan Reitman.

Starring Arnold Schwartzenegger, Danny DeVito, Kelly Preston.

THE SHORT STORY ★ Genetically-engineered "twins" are separated at birth, only to reunite 30 years later. The two couldn't be more dissimilar. One twin is built like Mr. Universe and has a sweet, mild nature. The other twin is shifty, short, and cranky. And yet, they connect. It's worth the price of a video rental just to see the mismatched Danny DeVito and Arnold Schwartzenegger walk down the street side by side.

MEMORABLE MOMENT ★ Seeing the really big Schwartzenegger in shorts and high-tops.

MESSAGE ★ When it comes to family, it's what's inside that counts.

Uncle Buck (1989)

Directed by John Hughes.

Starring John Candy, Amy Madigan, Jean Louisa Kelly.

THE SHORT STORY ★ John Candy stars in the title role as a crude, carefree slob who's forced to look after his brother's three kids when a family emergency arises. In addition to having girlfriend problems, Buck has a reputation for being allergic to responsibility. He bonds with his two younger relatives but 15-year-old Tia takes an immediate dislike to her new caretaker. A funny and sometimes poignant look at the adjustments we have to make in order to get along.

MEMORABLE LINE ★ After one of the kids ignores his instructions about meeting him, Uncle Buck says, "Stand me up today and I'll drive you to school in my robe and pyjamas and walk you to your first class."

MESSAGE ★ Tough love can be funny.

CHECK THIS OUT ★ If you want more Candy, try another John Hughes film, 1987's *Planes, Trains and Automobiles*.

Wayne's World (1992)

Directed by Penelope Spheeris.

Starring Mike Myers, Dana Carvey, Rob Lowe.

THE SHORT STORY ★ Based on a popular sketch from *Saturday Night Live*. Two dopey, long-haired slackers (Myers and Carvey as Wayne and Garth) have their own cable TV show. This film is aimless and silly, but also strangely endearing. You believe these two guys will be friends for life, probably because nobody else will have them. Warning: The 1993 sequel isn't nearly as much fun.

MEMORABLE LINE ★ "We're not worthy! We're not worthy!"

MESSAGE ★ Party on!

Who Framed Roger Rabbit (1988)

Directed by Robert Zemeckis.

Starring Bob Hoskins, Christopher Lloyd, Joanna Cassidy.

THE SHORT STORY ★ A dazzling mix of live action and animation, the plot blends the various cartoon citizens of 'Toon Town with assorted flesh-and-blood performers. After a while it's hard to tell which is which. Bob Hoskins stars as Eddie Valient, a tough-as- nails private eye who's hired to see if Roger Rabbit's 'Toon wife Jessica is cheating on her husband. Things get complicated from there. But this crazy ride never slows down. The result? You'll never look at cartoons the same way again.

MEMORABLE LINE ★ The sultry Jessica Rabbit's declaration "I'm not bad. I'm just drawn that way."

MESSAGE ★ Cartoon life can be just as complicated as the real thing.

Young Frankenstein (1974)

Directed by Mel Brooks.

Starring Gene Wilder, Peter Boyle, Teri Garr.

THE SHORT STORY ★ A high-spirited satire of one of the world's most enduring horror stories. The tale revolves around Dr. Frankenstein's grandson, Frederick (Wilder), who is intent on carrying on the family tradition of bringing a dead body back to life. Packed with great performances, but my personal favorite is Marty Feldman as the humpbacked Igor.

MEMORABLE MOMENT ★ Frankenstein's monster and a little girl playing on the seesaw together.

MESSAGE ★ Sometimes, you're better off dead.

Have You Seen These Classics?

Abbot and Costello Meet Frankenstein (1948)

Directed by Charles Barton.

Starring Bud Abbott, Lou Costello, Bela Lugosi.

THE SHORT STORY ★ If you've never checked out the comedy team of Abbott and Costello, treat yourself to this video. As an added bonus, you'll get a look at some of the scariest guys ever to hit the silver screen playing it for laughs. Proof that great comedy is timeless.

MEMORABLE MOMENT ★ Any time Lou flees in panic.

MESSAGE ★ Scary can be funny too.

Arsenic and Old Lace (1944)

Directed by Frank Capra.

Starring Cary Grant, Priscilla Lane, Raymond Massey.

THE SHORT STORY ★ Cary Grant's Mortimer Brewster is a nephew with a problem. His sweet maiden aunts are poisoning gentleman callers and burying them in the basement. And that's just the start of this darkly funny farce. The hilarious situation builds to such a feverish pitch that you don't know how director Capra can sustain the frantic pace. Don't worry about it. Just enjoy the roller coaster.

MEMORABLE MOMENT ★ On the subject of insanity running in his family, Mortimer quips, "It practically gallops."

MESSAGE ★ Don't feel left out just because you're sane and everybody else is crazy.

CHECK THIS OUT ★ For more classic Cary Grant, try 1938's *Holiday*.

Back to the Future (1985)

Directed by Robert Zemeckis.

Starring Michael J. Fox, Lea Thompson, Christopher Lloyd.

THE SHORT STORY ★ For teenaged slacker Marty McFly (Fox), the '80s are turning out to be a rough decade. He has family problems, school problems—you name it. So after his scientist pal Doc Brown (Lloyd) invents a time machine in the form of a DeLorean sports car, it's not all bad news when Marty is accidentally transported back to the year 1955. The problem? While stuck in the past, he disrupts the romantic destiny of his future parents. His mission? Bring them back together, or else Marty won't exist.

MEMORABLE LINE ★ As the eccentric Doc Brown, Christopher Lloyd points out the versatility of his time-traveling car with, "Roads? Where we're going we don't need roads."

MESSAGE ★ There's no time like the present.

Duck Soup (1933)

Directed by Leo McCary.

Starring The Marx Brothers, Margaret Dumont.

THE SHORT STORY ★ All of the Marx Brothers films have something to recommend them. But this legendary romp blends their patented craziness with a dash of political satire. Groucho plays the shifty Rufus T. Firefly, the leader of the mythical kingdom of Freedonia. Packed with classic comedy bits. Keep an eye out for the celebrated mirror scene.

MEMORABLE LINE ★ When the less-than-gorgeous Mrs. Teasdale informs Groucho's Firefly that she kissed her late husband before he died, he replies: "Oh, I see. Then it was murder."

MESSAGE ★ Never trust a leader. At least, not the ones in this movie.

Common theme

The theme song for *M*A*S*H — Suicide Is Painless* — was composed by director **Robert Altman's** teenaged son.

Monty Python's Life of Brian (1979)

Directed by Terry Jones.

Starring Graham Chapman, John Cleese, Terry Gilliam.

THE SHORT STORY ★ Only the Monty Python gang could do a satire based on the life of Christ and pull it off so beautifully. While some may find the antics of this British comedy troupe a bit much, they do expose various forms of religious hypocrisy in true Python style. A totally irreverent parable with a message tucked underneath all the laughs.

MEMORABLE MOMENT ★ The graffiti scene.

MESSAGE ★ Think for yourself.

CHECK THIS OUT ★ For some classic Monty Python sketches, see 1971's *And Now for Something Completely Different.*

National Lampoon's Animal House (1978)

Directed by John Landis.

Starring John Belushi, Tim Matheson, John Vernon.

THE SHORT STORY ★ A comic look at college fraternity life in the early '60s courtesy of the raucous Delta House. Welcome to a life of drinking beer, hanging out with your buddies, and avoiding academic responsibilities at all costs. Best remembered for John Belushi's inspired performance as Bluto, a tasteless slob bent on getting supreme revenge against the college's dictatorial dean. If higher education had really been like this, *nobody* would have graduated.

MEMORABLE MOMENT ★ Bluto's novel impression of a zit.

MESSAGE ★ If you move fast enough, irresponsibility has a tough time catching up with you.

The Odd Couple (1968)

Directed by Gene Saks.

Starring Jack Lemmon, Walter Matthau, Herb Edelman.

THE SHORT STORY ★ A must for anyone who has a friend with habits that drive them crazy. Two poker buddies attempt to share the same apartment after one of them is suddenly dumped by his wife. Oscar is a fun-loving slob whereas the neurotic Felix is compulsively neat. As far as living together goes, it's doomed from the start. But as a comedy, this one really delivers. The best part? After all these guys go through, you can tell they still like each other.

MEMORABLE MOMENT ★ When Felix explains the difference between spaghetti and linguini.

MESSAGE ★ Just because you like somebody doesn't mean you can share the same living space.

Special combination

Abbott and Costello formed one of the most successful comedy teams of all time. **Bud Abbott** was the rake-thin straight man while the short, rotund **Lou Costello** got most of the laughs with his crazy, slapstick antics. Their best films include their comedies where they encounter classic horror figures of the silver screen such as the Mummy. Few performers communicated sheer terror better than Costello. But, for all his scary moments, he died with a happy thought. His last words were reported as: "That was the best ice-cream soda I ever tasted."

The Party (1968)

Directed by Blake Edwards.

Starring Peter Sellers, Claudine Longet, Denny Miller.

THE SHORT STORY ★ A cult favorite. Peter Sellers plays a sweetly bumbling actor invited to a swank Hollywood party. A recipe for disaster and masterful slapstick. This is the movie that comes closest to showcasing Sellers's talent as a modern Charlie Chaplin. Funny without being mean-spirited. Don't miss it.

MEMORABLE MOMENT ★ The swimming pool scene.

MESSAGE ★ Next time, stay home.

Some Like It Hot (1959)

Directed by Billy Wilder.

Starring Jack Lemmon, Tony Curtis, Marilyn Monroe.

THE SHORT STORY ★ Two '20s jazz musicians find themselves in the wrong place at the wrong time. After witnessing a gangland slaying, Joe and Jerry must find a clever way to avoid vengeful mobsters. They decide to disguise themselves as women and join an all-female band until things cool off. The result is one of the funniest movies ever made. It's worth it just to watch nerdy Jerry (Lemmon) get carried away with his role as the good-time girl "Daphne."

MEMORABLE MOMENT ★ In his role as Daphne, Jerry has attracted the attention of a weathly suitor named Osgood. When "Daphne" confesses that he's actually a man, Osgood quips: "Well, nobody's perfect."

CHECK THIS OUT ★ Looking for another gender-switch comedy? Try Dustin Hoffman in 1982's *Tootsie*.

Take the Money and Run (1969)

Directed by Woody Allen.

Starring Woody Allen, Janet Margolin, Marcel Hillaire.

THE SHORT STORY ★ Woody Allen makes his directing debut as Virgil Starkwell, the world's most inept criminal. Virgil started to steal in order to pay for his cello lessons. From there, everything goes downhill. What can you say about a guy who robs 16 banks and gets 16 convictions? Unlike some of Allen's later films, this one's played strictly for laughs.

MEMORABLE MOMENT ★ The indecipherable bank note.

MESSAGE ★ Making an honest living couldn't be harder than this.

Index of Films

★ ★ ★ ★ ★

Index of Actors

Acknowledgements

I am indebted to a number of sources for both research and enlightenment. Standard sources such as *The Internet Movie Database, Leonard Maltin's Film and Video Guide* and *Emphriam Katz's Film Encyclopedia* have proved extremely helpful. I am especially indebted to *We'll Always Have Paris: The Definitive Guide to Great Lines from the Movies* by Robert and Gwendolyn Nowlan. In addition, I am deeply grateful for the advice, support and wisdom of my colleagues John Burns, Beth McArthur and Shelley Youngblut.

About the Author

John Lekich is a freelance writer who has been working as a journalist, movie reviewer and essayist for 18 years. His work has appeared in such publications as *Reader's Digest, The Los Angeles Times* and *The Hollywood Reporter.* John has won numerous magazine awards on subjects ranging from the arts and human rights issues to business and medicine.

As a movie critic, he has interviewed people on dozens of film sets. He had the honor of comparing noses with Steve Martin on the set of *Roxanne* and he once shared a beverage with George Plimpton. He was kissed by the legendary film actress Audrey Hepburn and believes he holds the record for the longest consecutive interview with novelist Michael Crichton.

John has co-written two feature-length screenplays and now adds to his list of accomplishments that of book author. In addition to *Reel Adventures: The Savvy Teens' Guide to Great Movies,* he is the author of a teen novel entitled *The Losers' Club.* He lives in Vancouver.